Jeff & Lori Jackson
10610 Sen... ...ich CT
0134

MAKE A
CHOICE

WHEN YOU ARE

AT THE INTERSECTION OF

Happiness and Despair

New York Times best-selling author
and award-winning journalist

JEFF BENEDICT

ENSIGN
PEAK

Interior photo: Shutterstock/© Andrey tiyk

© 2016 Jeff Benedict & Associates, LLC

Visit us at EnsignPeakPublishing.com

Library of Congress Cataloging-in-Publication Data
Names: Benedict, Jeff, author.
Title: Make a choice : when you are at the intersection of happiness and despair / Jeff
    Benedict.
Description: Salt Lake City, Utah : Ensign Peak, [2016] | ?2016
Identifiers: LCCN 2015049484 (print) | LCCN 2015051188 (ebook) | ISBN
    9781629721545 (hardbound : alk. paper) | ISBN 9781629734378 (ebook)
Subjects: LCSH: Choice (Psychology) | Happiness. | Conduct of life.
Classification: LCC BF611 .B46 2016 (print) | LCC BF611 (ebook) | DDC
    170/.44—dc23
LC record available at http://lccn.loc.gov/2015049484

Printed in the United States of America
Edwards Brothers Malloy, Ann Arbor, MI

10 9 8 7 6 5 4 3 2 1

To Basil

CONTENTS

ACKNOWLEDGMENTS

It wasn't my idea to write this book. A few years ago I received a call from Sheri Dew, the president and CEO of Ensign Peak. She reads my blog and suggested it might make for an inspiring book to expand some of the blog posts I'd written about people who had wrestled with pain, loss, and hardship. She didn't suggest any specific storylines or even offer a general outline. It was more of a hunch or gut feeling. But coming from Sheri, that was enough for me. In addition to being a friend, she is someone whose professional judgment and smarts I trust and admire.

I feel similarly about the product director for Ensign Peak, Chris Schoebinger. We've worked together previously, and he picked up Sheri's idea and ran with it. After I selected the individuals to profile, Chris helped refine each chapter, offering great input on the chapter setups and the takeaway messages. Chris is a writer's editor as well as a trusted friend and confidant.

Of course, this book would not exist without the courage of those who are profiled in it: Hugh, Ione, Bruce, Scott, Icy, Sargeant, Lindsay, Ben, Judith, Kev, Donna, Ri-Man, Mark, Kitam Sr., Kitam Jr., and Donyetta. It's a remarkable collection of people, all of whom were willing to discuss very personal and heart-wrenching experiences with me. Writing about them made me a better human.

I dedicated this book to my friend Basil. Back when I had never been published, Basil believed in me. He was my first literary agent. And I was his last client. After a storied career representing some of the biggest names in publishing, Basil stopped representing writers in order to care full time for his lovely wife, Nancy. Her illness robbed her of her mobility, but she has a man who loves her more than life. Basil hasn't left Nancy's side in years. Literally. Their love affair is the stuff of novels.

Basil is no longer my agent. But he remains my beloved friend. Without ever saying a word about love and marriage, he has taught me more about love and marriage than anyone I've ever met.

I've saved the most important acknowledgment for last. My wife, Lydia, is my best friend. She's also my best editor. I go to her with the big questions. In addition to helping me select the people I should profile, she had a hand in almost every one of the stories I told. She knows almost everyone in these pages. At one point, when I thought about giving up on the project, she rallied me and literally saved the book. I love writing, but I love Lydia way more.

INTRODUCTION

As a journalist I often meet people who have experienced fundamental unfairness, gut-wrenching loss, and outright injustice. This kind of news is everywhere; we see and hear about it every day.

Hours after I finished typing the final passage of this book and prepared to send the manuscript to my editor, a twenty-one-year-old white male entered a black church in South Carolina and killed nine people. *Why?* I was simultaneously furious and sad as I read the initial news reports.

That same night I read the final three chapters of *Old Yeller* to my nine-year-old daughter. We'd been reading a chapter a night for a couple of weeks, so she had a sense of what was coming. Still, it was all she could do not to cry when fourteen-year-old Travis puts a gun to his dog's head and pulls the trigger. It seems so unfair. After all, Old Yeller had saved Travis's life from a pack of wild hogs. Then he'd saved Travis's mother and brother from a ferocious wolf with rabies. Unfortunately, Old Yeller contracted rabies and had to be put down.

"Why did that have to happen?" my daughter asked.

It was her way of asking why the story didn't end differently. I couldn't help thinking of all the people in South Carolina who had lost loved ones. I was confident none of them imagined that a relative would die from gunfire in a church while studying the words of Christ. But author Fred Gipson teaches a very adult lesson in his children's classic. With Travis unable to get over the hurt of the tragic situation, his father tells him,

> "It's not a thing you can forget. I don't guess it's a thing you ought to forget. What I mean is, things like that happen. They may seem mighty cruel and unfair, but that's how life is a part of the time.
>
> "But that isn't the only way life is. A part of the time, it's mighty good. And a man can't afford to waste all the good part, worrying about the bad parts."

The Old Yeller scenario isn't a perfect comparison to what happened in South Carolina, but the reference to "mighty good" as a response to "cruel and unfair" was on display two days later when the shooter appeared on a video link in court during a bond hearing. Survivors of the victims addressed him. One of them was Nadine Collier. Her seventy-year-old mother, Ethel Lance, was among the victims. "You took something very precious away from me," Collier said. "I will never talk to her ever again. I will never be able to hold her again. But I forgive you." The next day, her words—'I Will Never Be Able to Hold Her Again. But I Forgive You'—were the headline atop the front page of the *New York Times*.

Losing a loved one in a random mass shooting is unimaginable, yet it has become too common in America. While writing this book, I had the privilege of working with Alissa Parker, whose daughter Emilie died in the Sandy Hook Elementary School shooting in Connecticut in 2012. Alissa asked me to help her write a memoir about going through the cruelest, most unfair thing a mother can experience and how she managed to forgive and move forward. Through a profound tragedy, she found the mighty good that still existed in the world.

The people and stories chronicled in this book remind me that life offers a rich diversity of hardships and personal trials. People wake up and face extraordinary circumstances every day. Maybe you're experiencing something hard right now. Maybe you wonder how you'll get over it. The fact is that we don't really get "over" these things. The only way is *through* them. However, there is strength and reassurance in knowing that we are not alone. The people profiled in these pages demonstrate that life is better when you focus on the mighty good and leave the bad parts behind.

Years ago I started a file and filled it with examples of people who chose to live an abundant life even when life handed them the worst. Most of the stories came from people I crossed paths with in my journalism career. These individuals represent a wide variety of religious denominations. They come from all around the country. Their stories show how everyday people—rich and poor, black and white, young and old—deal with the trials of life: misfortune, suffering, disaster, death, and hardship. These stories illustrate that we have a choice. Sure, it's easy to dwell on the cruel and the unfair, but we don't have to. Life is too short. Looking for the good can and will bless your life. It's blessed mine. And I'm a better person thanks to the individuals and families who've allowed me to tell these stories.

People wake up and face extraordinary circumstances every day. Maybe you're experiencing something hard right now. Maybe you wonder how you'll get over it. . . .

There is strength and reassurance in knowing that we are not alone. . . .

Life is better when you focus on the mighty good and leave the bad parts behind.

"We must develop and maintain the capacity to forgive. He who is devoid of the power to forgive is devoid of the power to love. There is some good in the worst of us and some evil in the best of us. When we discover this, we are less prone to hate our enemies."

—MARTIN LUTHER KING JR.

CHAPTER ONE

CHOOSE TO FORGIVE

In 1957, Martin Luther King Jr. delivered a Christmas sermon at the Dexter Avenue Baptist Church titled "Loving Your Enemies." In it he said, "We must develop and maintain the capacity to forgive. He who is devoid of the power to forgive is devoid of the power to love. There is some good in the worst of us and some evil in the best of us. When we discover this, we are less prone to hate our enemies."

Truer words have seldom been spoken. They are hard to live by but worthy of our best effort. This is a story about a neighbor of mine who demonstrates that even in the most overwhelming circumstances, forgiveness is still a choice.

• • •

In 2007, my family purchased an old farmhouse in rural Virginia. It sits at the end of a dirt lane. A few years after we moved in, one of our vehicles was towed to a garage for repairs. In need of a temporary replacement, I called Enterprise, the only car rental agency in the area. Soon an Enterprise driver in his late sixties showed up at my home. He greeted me with a smile and introduced himself as Hugh.

He looked familiar, but I couldn't place him. Maybe it was his close resemblance to Gordon Jump, the actor-turned-Maytag pitchman. Anyway, I hopped in and asked if he'd had any trouble finding my place. He laughed. "No," he said. "I'm your neighbor." As we neared the end of my half-mile-long driveway, he pointed to his house—the one with the immaculate lawn.

"Now I know why you look familiar," I told him. "I always see you on your riding lawnmower."

He laughed again. "That's me," he said. Then he went on about how much he enjoyed working in his yard.

I asked how long he'd been driving for Enterprise.

A few years, he said. It gave him something to do in retirement. Plus, he said, he enjoyed driving new vehicles and meeting new people.

Fifteen minutes later we were at the car lot. I made a point to tell the desk agent that Hugh had an infectious smile. The agent agreed. Then he asked, "You know about Hugh's background?"

I shrugged my shoulders. Hugh was a neighbor, but I'd known him less than an hour. His background was a mystery.

The agent lowered his voice. A long time ago, he told me, Hugh's wife was shot and killed. It was an accident. They had just left their church. She died in the parking lot. Hugh had been a widower ever since.

> Every time we talked, I came away with the same impression—the guy was chronically happy.

Over the next few years, Hugh drove me to or from Enterprise whenever I rented a car. Every time we talked, I came away with the same impression—the guy was chronically happy. I'd think the same thing each time I saw him riding his mower. He'd smile and wave. His apparent outlook on life seemed in such sharp contrast to the story I'd been told.

Intrigued, I paid a visit to the office of the local newspaper and requested permission to look through the stacks. Eventually I came across this front-page headline: "Woman Dies in Shooting." Under it there were two photographs, one of a shattered car window and one of a bullet hole in the side of a pickup truck. There were two stories: "Gun Fired by Child in Church Lot," and "Victim Was Active in Church."

On November 24, 1991, Hugh and his wife, Linda, had attended an evening worship service at a local Baptist church, where they were longtime members of the congregation. Linda taught Sunday school there and cared for the children in the nursery. After the services concluded, they stuck around for a going-away reception for a family leaving the area. It was about 9:45 p.m. when Hugh helped his wife and thirteen-year-old daughter into the family car.

They had parked alongside a pickup truck that belonged to a young couple with a three-year-old son. The boy's father, a hunter, kept a 12-gauge shotgun on the gun rack in the cab. As the family prepared to leave, the boy's mother opened the driver's side door and hoisted the toddler up onto the seat. While the mother walked around to the passenger's side, the boy reached for the gun and pulled the trigger, causing a deafening blast. A slug tore through the passenger's side of the cab, shattering Hugh's driver's side window just as he leaned forward to put the key in the ignition.

Then came the screams. Flying glass sprayed Hugh's daughter, drawing blood from her face and head. Linda cried out as Hugh rushed around to the passenger's side door. While he tended to his daughter, he realized that his wife had slumped over in the middle seat. The slug had hit her in the face before landing under a Bible on the floor. Linda died at the scene. She was forty-five.

During the subsequent police investigation into the shooting, details revealed that the previous day, the father of the toddler had taken his little boy deer hunting on a farm.

At the end of the hunt, he'd purposely left one cartridge in the chamber just in case he and his son came across a deer as they were leaving. He'd forgotten to remove it. Just as he had forgotten to engage the safety mechanism.

Hugh was devastated, and his daughter was traumatized. She required twenty stitches to her head from the cuts caused by the glass fragments. Worse, she had lost her mother. The courts provided no relief. At the time, it was legal to carry a loaded gun in a motor vehicle. Linda's senseless death would go unpunished. The gun owner ended up pleading no contest to "recklessly leaving a loaded, unsecured firearm in such a manner as to endanger life and limb of any child under the age of fourteen." Hugh testified at the man's sentencing. "She started hollering that she'd been hit," he said before he broke down and wept. "I looked at my wife . . . she was gone."

> Hugh broke down and wept. "I looked at my wife . . . she was gone."

The judge imposed the maximum sentence—a $500 fine.

After I'd read the news accounts on the accident, I got up the nerve to ask Hugh how he'd managed to maintain such a cheerful outlook on life. He started telling me about his wife. It was the first time he had ever mentioned her. His trademark smile faded as he recounted the details of that fateful night in the church parking lot. Tears streamed down his cheeks. Twenty-three years had passed, but the anguish over her absence was still just beneath the surface.

I asked how he managed not to be bitter or angry or depressed.

He said he had been all of those things at the time of the incident, and he'd remained that way through a fruitless effort to get the gun laws in his county changed. Then he'd gotten involved in a lawsuit against the gun manufacturer, but that didn't turn out well either. Hugh couldn't find peace—until he decided to accept and forgive. To honor his wife, he chose to live the rest of his life as she had lived hers—with ill will toward none.

> Hugh couldn't find peace—until he decided to accept and forgive.

As he told me these things, it occurred to me that my wife was the same age his was at the time of the accident. I also had a thirteen-year-old child. I wondered how I would have held up had I been in Hugh's shoes. Not nearly as well, I suspected.

I asked if he was ever tempted to blame or question God.

He wiped his eyes. No, he told me. Never. Faith was something he and his wife had in common. Those shared beliefs helped him realize that the other family had suffered too. The father had to live with the knowledge that his mistake had led to a toddler taking an innocent woman's life.

Hugh got to a point where he felt empathy for the other family, not anger.

Rather than dwell on it, he stayed busy. Friendships and a sense of purpose kept him going. He enjoyed working in his yard. He liked to drive around and meet new people. He still went to church. He smiled a lot.

Forgiveness is not the most obvious choice in dire circumstances, but it's a choice nonetheless. Hugh's example is a testament to Martin Luther King Jr.'s words and to the power of choosing the mighty good. As we forgive others, we acknowledge that there is some good in all of us, and we are freed to more fully love and lift those around us.

> Forgiveness is not the most obvious choice in dire circumstances, but it's a choice nonetheless.

"The important thing is to teach a child that good can always triumph over evil."

—WALT DISNEY

CHAPTER TWO

CHOOSE TO GIVE
SECOND CHANCES

Walt Disney once said, "The important thing is to teach a child that good can always triumph over evil." It is a theme that runs through so many classic Disney films. It's a theme I try to instill in my daughters when I read them bedtime stories. But in my career as a journalist, I encounter stories—real life stories—where evil sometimes triumphs over good. That's where Disney's words "Teach a child that good *can* always triumph over evil" come in. *Can* indicates we have a say in the matter. This is a story about a friend who let good triumph by giving an enemy a second chance.

• • •

I was nineteen when I left home in Connecticut to begin my Mormon mission in Seattle in 1985. My first two months were spent with Bruce Jasper, a twenty-year-old missionary from Logan, Utah, who taught me the ropes and helped me acclimate to missionary life. One of the first things he did was take me to the local supermarket. We were walking back to our apartment with armloads of grocery bags when a car full of college-age boys approached. In our white shirts, ties, and name badges, it was easy to tell we were missionaries. The car slowed down just long enough for the guys to throw open containers of beer at us. Our shirts and food got soaked. I wanted to fight. Bruce just shrugged it off.

That wasn't the only way he and I were different. He'd been born and raised a Mormon and had never been back East. I had been baptized in the Catholic church and later converted to Mormonism. I knew little about Utah. Besides the fact that we were both serving missions, it seemed like the only thing we had in common was our mutual love of basketball. Nonetheless, he became my best friend in Seattle. After living with him, I wished I had some of his personality traits. He was patient and not easily provoked. He was the kind of guy who wouldn't step on a spider. He read the Bible every night before bed, but he never preached. Not to me. Not to anyone. People on the fringes of society liked to be around him because he made them feel accepted.

We remained close after completing our missions. I got

to know his wife and children, and he got to know mine. Anytime I visited Utah on business, we made an effort to get together. This went on for years. Then, on one occasion, I was doing a series of public appearances in Salt Lake City and Provo in connection with a book I had recently published. Bruce tagged along with me for the day. At one point we were walking from one event to another, and he told me how much he admired me. Then he confided that he had long wished he were more like me in my overall approach to life. There was a subtle sadness in his voice. We were in our early forties at that point, and Bruce had been through a divorce, among other things. I didn't know what to say. So I put my arms around him, and he squeezed me like he didn't want to let go.

A couple years later, in the early part of 2010, I received a package from Bruce's mother, Ione. Whenever I visited their home, she treated me like a son. More than once I told Bruce that he had the most thoughtful mother on earth. I remember being intrigued by her package.

> More than once I told Bruce that he had the most thoughtful mother on earth.

What could she be sending me? The first thing I removed from the parcel was a funeral notice. *Who died?* I wondered. Then I found a card. It contained an obituary. I was speechless when I realized it was Bruce's. It gave no clue as to the cause of death. I immediately assumed cancer or some other terminal illness. Why hadn't he told me? What had happened?

I called Ione. The story that emerged was filled with loss, but also with hope. It began on November 13, 2008.

That day, Ione's husband, John, passed away in their Smithfield, Utah, home. After forty-eight years of marriage, nothing was the same. Her best friend was gone. The house felt empty.

Fortunately, she had Bruce around. Divorced and living alone, Bruce had moved back in with his parents a couple years earlier after contracting MRSA, a potentially deadly staph bacteria resistant to antibiotics. He had worked in the health care industry as an occupational therapist, but complications from his infection had disabled him. All of his top teeth abscessed and had to be removed. Barely able to eat, he lost weight and his muscles deteriorated. His parents had taken him in, hoping to lift his spirits, but his physical limitations discouraged him. A certified lifeguard and long-distance marathon runner, he'd always been strong and active. Suddenly he couldn't walk to the car without pain.

By the time his father died, Bruce had regained some strength. Though still struggling, he shifted all of his focus to his mother. His objective was to keep her occupied. He did it through little things: Telling her inspiring stories about the patients he'd met during his years as a therapist. Having lunch with her. Helping her do family history research on the computer. Telling her he loved her. Mostly, though, he simply stayed by her side. Company, he had learned through firsthand experience, was the best way to get a person through loneliness.

Only five short months after losing her husband, Ione suffered another tragic loss.

On April 22, 2009, her eighteen-year-old grandson, Derek Jasper, and his best friend were driving home one evening after a church activity. At an intersection in Ogden, a Cadillac doing eighty miles an hour ran a red light and plowed into them, causing an explosion. Derek and his friend died on impact.

The Cadillac was driven by a seventeen-year-old gang member with a lengthy criminal record. The police had been pursuing him in connection with a home invasion when he'd sped through the red light. He was knocked unconscious by the crash and taken into custody, where his blood-alcohol level was determined to be twice the legal limit. His twenty-one-year-old cousin, also a gang member, was in the passenger's seat. Escaping injury, he attempted to flee the scene on foot and fought with police. He was convicted for assaulting a police officer and sentenced to 120 days in jail. The driver faced two counts of automobile homicide.

> Company, he had learned through firsthand experience, was the best way to get a person through loneliness.

Ione's family and the other victim's family mourned for

weeks. Derek was an Eagle Scout and had been just weeks away from leaving on a two-year mission for the Mormon church. His friend had been a college student who coached lacrosse at a local high school. After the accident, members of both boys' families suffered insomnia, panic attacks, and depression.

Derek and his friend had a reputation for being peacemakers. They weren't the type to espouse hatred or seek revenge. To honor their memory, both families attended the driver's sentencing and requested mercy, not retribution.

> To honor their memory, both families attended the driver's sentencing and requested mercy, not retribution.

"We hope some good will come out of this," Derek's mother told the judge. "We hope the driver takes every opportunity to become a good citizen and member of society."

The other victim's mother said essentially the same thing.

Their forgiveness overwhelmed the driver's family. "I don't know how they can do that," his aunt said. "But it was everything for them to forgive them for what happened."

The judge was moved too. "I'm so impressed with the families of these victims, who seem to bear no anger toward you but a sense of forgiveness," he told the accused. "I hope you will find that inspiring and you will dignify their confidence in you."

He then sentenced the young man to consecutive prison terms of one to fifteen years.

Ione had found it in her heart to extend a second chance to someone who needed it. She became an example to Bruce, who would find himself facing a similar decision only a few months later when a series of tragic circumstances happened to him.

On October 3, 2009, Bruce told his mother he was taking off for the day. It was a Saturday, and he wanted to try out a new archery set he had purchased. She told him to enjoy himself and be careful; she'd see him when he returned.

Bruce drove about two hours through scenic Logan Canyon to Bear Lake. A nature lover and lifelong camper, he spent the day exploring trails. He ended up at the north end of Bear Lake Valley in Montpelier, Idaho, a town of three thousand. With daylight fading, he found a motel for the night. Then he headed out for a bite to eat at Butch Cassidy Restaurant and Saloon. While eating, he saw a much younger man verbally harassing a waitress.

> Ione had found it in her heart to extend a second chance to someone who needed it.

"That's no way to talk to a lady," Bruce said.

According to witness accounts, when Bruce left the restaurant, the younger man followed him out and punched him in the back of the head. Bruce dropped like a felled tree, his face slamming onto the concrete walkway. Bleeding profusely from the head, his pulse faded rapidly and he lost consciousness. The next thing he remembered was waking up at Logan Regional Hospital after undergoing six hours of emergency plastic surgery. Metal plates were inserted around his eyes. His shattered nasal bones were reset.

Ione got a call at home in the middle of the night. It was all she could do to keep it together when she saw Bruce's swollen, disfigured, and bandaged face. He was unrecognizable. His vital signs were still weak. He was near death.

The man who attacked Bruce was apprehended at the scene and charged with a felony—aggravated battery—meaning the battery had resulted in great bodily harm and permanent disability. He was twenty-three and already on probation for burglary. Turns out his juvenile years had been tragically sad. If convicted for attacking Bruce, his adult years would be spent behind bars. However, the prosecutor could recommend a six-month stint in a substance-abuse facility, which would require vacating his burglary conviction. As the victim, Bruce would have an opportunity to tell the court how he felt about the proposed alternative sentencing.

For a while, Bruce was in no condition to talk to anyone. After his initial surgery, he spent two months in and out of the hospital dealing with chronic infections and other complications stemming from the injuries. For example, one of the metal plates beneath his eyes slipped through the roof of his mouth, causing a hole that resulted in infection. One eye never blinked after the assault, and his speech was slurred. Embarrassed by his appearance and his inability to put words together, he didn't want to face family and friends.

Eventually Bruce talked to his mother and his attorney about his assailant's upcoming hearing. Convinced he wasn't going to live much longer, Bruce confided that he didn't want to die with malice in his heart. "Whether I make it through this is not as important as what I can do to help this young man turn his life around," Bruce told them.

Despite a paralyzing headache and dizziness, Bruce traveled with his family to Idaho for the hearing. He told the court that he supported leniency. Treatment, he said, was preferable to incarceration. Bruce's thinking was clear—he had enjoyed an ideal upbringing with loving parents and opportunities to grow and thrive; the guy who'd attacked him had none of that.

> "Whether I make it through this is not as important as what I can do to help this young man turn his life around," Bruce told them.

"Bruce wanted to try and help this kid turn his life around," Ione said. "Getting him into that treatment program was a better option than putting him behind bars for many years."

The court went along with Bruce's wishes and sentenced the twenty-three-year-old to six months in treatment. However, if the young man did not meet the treatment requirements and satisfy all the terms of his probation, he'd serve the full prison term for his burglary plus additional years for the attack on Bruce.

Weeks later, Bruce and Ione were in the family room. It was January 14, 2010, and the Utah Jazz were on television. Bruce lay motionless on the couch. The pain had become unbearable, and he hadn't eaten much in the last forty-eight hours. When the game ended, Bruce sat up.

"Mom, I'm so tired."

"Let's have prayer and go to bed. I'll say it."

"No. I want to pray."

From the couch, he struggled to get the words out. He thanked Jesus Christ for His example and all He had done for mankind. He expressed gratitude for the privilege of being a missionary when he was nineteen. He also thanked God for his family and friends, and he asked for a blessing on them. Then he prayed for his assailant. It took him an hour to get it all out. Ione wiped away tears. She'd never heard him pour out his soul like that.

> He also thanked God for his family and friends, and he asked for a blessing on them. Then he prayed for his assailant.

Then he struggled to his feet and embraced her. "I love you, Mom," he whispered. "I don't know if I'll be here in the morning," he continued. "I am *so* tired."

A few hours later, Bruce died in his sleep. He was forty-four.

. . .

Within a nine-month period, Ione had lost a son and a grandson due to random acts of violence committed by young men with criminal records. Agonized by her losses, she nonetheless refused to become bitter.

The Sunday following Bruce's death, Ione attended her church to play the organ for her fellow worshippers. She was going through the most difficult trial of her life, and she wanted desperately to be around people of faith.

She had been a vocalist, choir accompanist, and organist for her Mormon congregation for over fifty-five years, never receiving a penny in compensation. Her payment, she said, was the satisfaction that came with serving others. Her music inspired people, and it gave her a sense of purpose.

> "In life, it isn't what happens to us that matters," she said. "It's what we do with it. You don't give up on your faith. You incorporate it into your life as life happens."

"In life, it isn't what happens to us that matters," she said. "It's what we do with it. You don't give up on your faith. You incorporate it into your life as life happens."

Still, there were long, lonely days that followed. And when those lonely days came, she'd pull out a gift Bruce had left her—his journals. Bruce had been a prolific journal writer. Reading his entries was like getting to know her son all over again. Ione discovered lots of things she didn't know. "It was a deep insight into his soul," she said. "He was so revealing in what he wrote."

Bruce had continued to write even after he was attacked and underwent surgery. One evening Ione flipped to Bruce's last journal entry, written the day before he died. By that point it was difficult for him to see well enough to construct letters legibly or have the strength to grip a pen. The entry looked like something a toddler might have scratched out. But Ione made out the short sentences: *"Oh, goodness! I'm very blessed, and very 'worn out.' Know I love you eternally! I did the best with what I have had. Eternally, Bruce."*

> "He reminded me that when hard things happen to us, we shouldn't think it's the end. It's important that no matter what happens to us in life we follow our dreams."

Ione cried. "He left me a treasure," she said. "My love and admiration for him increased with each page. He reminded me that when hard things happen to us, we shouldn't think it's the end. It's important that no matter what happens to us in life we follow our dreams."

Weeks after Bruce Jasper's death, Ione received a thank-you letter from the Utah eye bank. Bruce was an organ donor, and the eye that had been protected by the eyelid that never blinked properly after the attack had been sent overseas and had given sight to someone else. A short while later Ione received a second letter, this time from a young woman who had been unable to walk due to a deformed anklebone.

One of Bruce's was surgically installed, giving her the ability to walk. "Sometimes it takes a while," Ione said. "But good does overcome evil."

> "Sometimes it takes a while," Ione said. "But good does overcome evil."

I opened this chapter with a quote from Walt Disney about the importance of teaching a child that good can triumph over evil. Certainly Ione did that in the way she raised Bruce. And Bruce's choice teaches us the power of choosing to give someone—especially someone who has wronged us—a second chance.

"What is the use in living, if it be not to strive for noble causes and to make this muddled world a better place for those who will live in it after we are gone?"

—WINSTON CHURCHILL

CHAPTER THREE

CHOOSE TO SERVE OTHERS

Winston Churchill's greatest genius may have been his ability to inspire others to serve during dark times. He made it sound so noble, so invigorating. He once said, "What is the use in living, if it be not to strive for noble causes and to make this muddled world a better place for those who will live in it after we are gone? How else can we put ourselves in harmonious relation with the great verities and consolations of the infinite and the eternal? And I avow my faith that we are marching towards better days. Humanity will not be cast down. We are going on swinging bravely forward along the grand high road and already behind the distant mountains is the promise of the sun."

Churchill spoke for a nation, but his words are

applicable to us as individuals. This chapter tells the story of a husband and wife who swung bravely forward amidst heartbreaking sorrow by choosing to serve others.

. . .

In 2011, I gave a speech in Connecticut about politics and the law. Afterward, I was greeting people from the audience when a man in a business suit approached, shook my hand, and introduced himself as Scott Frantz. He thanked me for my remarks, and I complimented his tie, which had the words *We the people* woven into the fabric. He flipped it over and showed me the designer label: Vineyard Vines. I was unfamiliar with the brand. He told me it was a new line launched by two brothers who'd quit their jobs and started making ties. "I'll send you one," he said.

Brief encounters seldom provide sufficient time to get to know someone, but I instantly liked Frantz's vibe. He seemed so at peace with himself and the world. We exchanged business cards. It wasn't until I glanced at his card that I realized he was a state senator. He downplayed his political title when I asked him about it. That made me like him even more. After he had rushed off to another appointment, a friend told me that he had deep admiration for Frantz. When I asked why, my friend said that Frantz and his wife had recently lost a one-year-old son to a rare disease.

I couldn't help thinking, *That guy?* He looked so happy, so full of life.

My friend told me that I should really get to know Frantz. He said that after losing his son, Frantz had basically dedicated his life to serving others through the state legislature and by increasing his service through nonprofit charities. His wife, Icy, had done something equally inspiring. She'd written a children's book designed to help families cope with the loss of a child, the proceeds of which went to families in need.

The more I heard, the more I wished I had a reason to reconnect with Frantz. About a week later, a box from Vineyard Vines arrived at my home. It contained a brand-new *We the people* tie. I hadn't really expected him to send me a tie. When I e-mailed him to say thank you, I asked about his wife, Icy, and her book.

He put me in touch with her, and I ended up writing a blog post about them and the loss of their son. When I asked Icy if she ever felt tempted to blame God, she said never. "I am religious, and I prayed for a miracle that he'd get better," she told me. "But I was blessed to have witnessed a lot of miracles that happened around him, although not the one that I was looking for. Our son changed people. We feel he came here for a reason and he did what he came here to do."

"I was blessed to have witnessed a lot of miracles that happened around him, although not the one that I was looking for."

Parents who lose a child often end up being defined by that tragedy. Not Scott and Icy. As our friendship grew and our families began to spend time together, I recognized that their ability to look outward instead of inward had a lot to do with the peace of mind they achieved in the aftermath of sorrow.

· · ·

Scott Frantz seldom played with toys when he was a boy. He was too busy learning to sail and fly. His father, Lee, owned both a marina on Long Island Sound and the Dutch airline Transavia, which had a satellite headquarters in nearby New York City. Scott often tagged along with his father at the shipyard and spent his summers boat racing and sailing in nearby coves, but his first love was aviation. He took his first flight before kindergarten, and his father let him take the controls of a plane when he was eleven. Scott dreamed of becoming a pilot.

Scott's older brother, Ted, and Scott's twin brother, Chris, had the same dream. Much of it had to do with their upbringing. The Frantz boys grew up in Greenwich, Connecticut. Their coastal home overlooked a tiny six-acre island that served as a year-round playground for the boys. The only other house on the island was an old Victorian, home to a bunch of American Airlines pilots. One of them was Leo Loudenslager, the only person to win seven national aerobatic titles.

Loudenslager was in his mid-twenties when he moved next door to the Frantzes. In 1967, Loudenslager started building an aerobatic plane. A number of his pilot friends worked on it with him, including flying ace Jim Roberts. Scott was seven at the time. His older brother Ted was nine. Loudenslager invited them to work alongside him and the other pilots. Scott's mother, Ann, liked the idea of her boys spending time with the airmen. She encouraged her boys to work hard and learn all they could.

Over the next five years, Scott spent hundreds of hours around the pilots and working on the plane. But it never felt like work. It was more like a boyhood wonderland. Scott was twelve when the Laser 200 was completed. Loudenslager won all of his United States Aerobatic Championships in it and ultimately the World Championship. Eventually, the plane was donated to the Smithsonian. It's on permanent display in the museum's Steven F. Udvar-Hazy Center.

Scott's childhood seemed idyllic. His father took him sailing and flying. His mother encouraged him to dream big, and she taught him the value of education. He attended a private grammar school and a boarding school before going off to Princeton. At twenty-two he had a degree and his pilot's license. By the spring of 1986, he was finishing up his MBA at Dartmouth. Then everything changed.

May 23, 1986, began as the perfect day—blue sky, warm temperatures, sunny. Scott was on Nantucket for a weekend getaway before his final exams. That afternoon, his twin brother, Chris, and a couple of friends were supposed to arrive in Nantucket for a fishing trip. Chris, a commercial helicopter pilot, was transporting his friends in his helicopter, a Bell 206 JetRanger. They planned to depart from a hangar in Stamford, Connecticut. But by sundown there was no sign of them.

Concerned, Lee Frantz checked with the hangar in Stamford and got confirmation that his son had departed from there earlier that day. Next, Scott and his dad called all the regional airports between Connecticut and the Cape. None had any record of a Bell 206-JetRanger landing. By the next day, Scott and his family couldn't help but think the worst. A Federal Aviation Administration computer radar printout showed an image that resembled a helicopter dropping off the screen near Westerly, Rhode Island. It was looking more and more like Chris had crashed. Scott's parents couldn't bear the thought.

Neither could Scott. He dropped everything and focused all his energy on finding his brother. The Massachusetts Civil Air Patrol and U.S. Coast Guard searched a six-thousand-square-mile area from the Connecticut coastline to just south of Cape Cod. After two weeks, nothing turned up and the search was discontinued. Determined, Scott and his family turned to the Woods Hole Oceanographic Institution, the world's leading private organization for oceanic exploration. A year earlier, oceanographers from Woods Hole had discovered the *Titanic* under twelve thousand feet of water near Newfoundland. The luxury liner had been lost for seventy-three years. Scott figured if anyone could find his brother's chopper it was these guys.

A base of operations was established at a small regional airport in Rhode Island not far from where the FAA last recorded a series of radar blips before the helicopter disappeared. Then, in mid-June, some fishermen off Martha's Vineyard found large fragments of blue-and-white fiberglass. One of the pieces had a serial number. It matched the number on the missing helicopter. For the next month oceanographers combed the area with military-grade sonar equipment. They turned up many more pieces of the helicopter. Then they found the bodies.

The challenge of trying to find his brother had given Scott a sense of purpose. It was also a distraction from facing the inevitable—that his brother wasn't coming back. That was over, though. Reality had arrived. And with it came sleeplessness. Alone in the dark, he'd toss and turn amidst the memories—teaching his brother to fly, taking him sailing, seeing the way Chris had lit up when he'd obtained his pilot's license. Yesterday seemed so far away. His eyes would well with tears, and he'd bury his face in his hands. He repeated this routine for weeks.

Scott laid his brother to rest near his home on a spit of land that jutted out into Long Island Sound. Scott's mother never recovered from the loss. She was diagnosed with cancer in 1988 and died just months later.

Within two and a half years, Scott had lost both his brother and his mother. He dealt with the loss by working fifteen-hour days, six days a week at a Wall Street firm doing mergers and acquisitions. He kept so busy he didn't have time to deal with his emotions. The money poured in, but he felt empty inside. On Christmas Eve in 1988, he was sitting at his desk at Bankers Trust, working on another deal, when he started to wonder, *What am I doing here? I should be helping the hungry or the homeless. There is so much more to life.*

> "When going through adversity, it is important to let your emotions out," Scott now advises. "It is critical not to hold back. In my case it was also critical that I focus on something positive and constructive."

"When going through adversity, it is important to let your emotions out," Scott now advises. "It is critical not to hold back. In my case it was also critical that I focus on something positive and constructive."

That night he pledged to leave Wall Street within three months.

He was gone in two. Early in 1989 he started his own investment firm not far from his childhood home in Greenwich, Connecticut. As a tribute to his younger brother, he helped establish a teen center in town, one of Chris's early ambitions. He also volunteered on numerous AmeriCares missions, making airlifts to Bosnia and Chechnya. But the best thing that happened to him was falling in love with Allison Hanley.

Like Scott, Allison had grown up in Greenwich and attended private schools, including an Episcopalian boarding school in New Hampshire. After college she had returned to Greenwich to work with Freedom Institute and Greenwich Academy as a drug-and-alcohol-prevention educator. Her nickname was Icy, but she was warm, down-to-earth, compassionate, and adventurous. Scott was smitten.

Scott and Icy married at Christ Church in Greenwich on December 18, 1993. He was thirty-three. She was twenty-eight. By 2000 they had three boys: a four year-old and a set of three-year-old twins. They settled next to Scott's childhood home on the six-acre island. After the old Victorian was demolished, he built a home there in 1991. His three sons were growing up the

They named the baby William, but they called him by his middle name—Sargeant.

way Scott and his brothers had, around sailboats and airplanes. Things seemed pretty idyllic. Icy was even pregnant again and expecting another son.

But in her eighth month of pregnancy, an ultrasound revealed that the baby wasn't moving as it should. Doctors induced labor, and Icy gave birth on September 28, 2000. They named the baby William, but they called him by his middle name—Sargeant, after the name of the second highest mountain in Maine's Acadia National Park.

Right away Icy knew something was different about Sargeant. For one thing, he never cried, not even when the nurse pricked his finger for a blood test. He didn't eat as much as her first three babies had, plus he slept constantly.

At first Icy figured she just had a very mellow baby. But when Sargeant was seven weeks old, he started having more serious issues. More than once Scott turned him over and patted his back, thinking Sargeant was choking. Then he had what appeared to be a seizure.

Concerned, they brought him to Greenwich Hospital. Blood samples were taken. Tests were conducted. Specialists were brought in. Ultimately Scott and Icy were told that their infant son was suffering from a mitochondrial disease.

What did that mean?

Scott and Icy wanted answers.

Doctors explained that there were hundreds of different mitochondrial diseases. Each disorder produced a similar set of symptoms: loss of motor skills, muscle weakness, swallowing difficulties, poor growth, respiratory complications, and seizures.

As was often the case with this illness, it was unclear precisely which strain was ailing Sargeant. But it was clear that his cells weren't producing enough energy.

What could be done?

The doctors did their best to couch it, but there was no cure for most mitochondrial diseases.

For Scott, it was like hearing that his brother's helicopter had disappeared off the coast of Rhode Island all over again. Only this was harder. Sargeant was only two months old. His life had barely begun.

Icy wept.

Giving up on Sargeant was not an option. Scott and Icy contacted the leading experts on mitochondrial diseases. They had Sargeant examined by a leading neurologist. They tried different treatments and visited numerous pediatric hospitals. They even sent a sample of Sargeant's tissue to Australia for advanced testing. But neither medicine nor science had an answer.

By Sargeant's first birthday, Icy realized his future was in God's hands. She prayed for a miracle that he'd get better, and then she dedicated every day to making Sargeant as comfortable as possible.

Scott prayed too, but he figured he wasn't going to get the outcome he wanted. "Losing my brother gave me the experience to know that I could survive losing a child," Scott said. "That being said, I still couldn't believe I was going through what I was going through. But I knew we could get through it."

. . .

It was a forty-five minute drive from Greenwich to Yale–New Haven Hospital. Icy prayed the entire way. Sargeant had been in the ICU for a number of weeks. But there was a slim chance he'd be able to come home for Christmas 2001. It would depend on whether the carbon dioxide levels in his blood were low enough. Too much CO_2 caused lethargy. "Please, God," Icy prayed. "Just let him pass his CO_2 test so he can come home. Please."

The moment Icy entered the ICU, she sensed that her prayer had been answered. The nurse greeted her with a big smile. "You're not going to believe it," she said.

"What?" Icy said.

"We did the CO_2 test, and his levels were lower than ever."

"Really?"

"Yes! Sargeant can go home."

Icy's eyes welled with tears. She threw her arms around the nurse, then wiped her cheeks. Sargeant was coming home for Christmas.

Then the doctor entered the room. He wasn't smiling. "I've ordered another test," he said.

Wait, why? she wondered.

He apologized but said he didn't trust the results. Before

releasing Sargeant, he wanted to be certain the readings were accurate.

Icy felt ill. A short while later the results from the second blood test came back telling a different story. The CO_2 levels in Sargeant's blood were far too high for him to leave the hospital.

Icy didn't get it. She had prayed fervently. She had gotten the result she wanted. And now the doctor was saying the first result was a false positive?

The forty-five-minute drive home seemed like hours. She felt like it was her will against God's will. It didn't seem fair. Why couldn't God answer her pleas?

> "The miracle we wanted— for him to get better— we didn't get, but there were so many other miracles we got that we didn't ask for."

All Icy wanted was for Sargeant to come home for Christmas. Instead, Icy's mother spent Christmas morning in the ICU with Sargeant so Icy and Scott could remain at home with the other children. A group calling itself Anonymous Angels left gifts at the Frantzes' home.

Then something dawned on Icy. "There were so many miracles happening around this child," she said. "The miracle we wanted—for him to get better—we didn't get, but there were so many other miracles we got that we didn't ask for."

• • •

A bird made a nest in the Christmas wreath on Scott and Icy's front door, so they decided to leave the wreath up well past the holidays. They even put up a sign telling people to use another entrance. In the spring the bird laid four eggs. The first three hatched. The fourth didn't. Icy considered it more than coincidence. It felt like God was trying to tell her something.

Right around the time the baby birds left the nest, Sargeant passed away. It was April 2002. He was eighteen months old. Scott and Icy buried him on the grounds of their church in Greenwich. Scott had Chris's grave moved next to Sargeant's. "I wanted them to be together," Scott said.

It was a difficult time. Scott had lost a brother and then a son for reasons that were hardly clear.

> Scott figured he had two choices: to be bitter and ask why, or to honor his brother and his son by helping others in need.

The cause of the crash was never determined. The cause of the mitochondrial disease was never found. Scott figured he had two choices: to be bitter and ask why, or to honor his brother and his son by helping others in need.

He reached out to the Corporate Angel Network, a charitable organization that uses empty seats on corporate jets to transport cancer patients to distant treatment centers.

Scott had recently bought a small jet and was looking to log as many flight hours as possible. He told the network he'd fly any cancer patients under the age of twelve on an as-needed basis. His goal was to ensure that no ill child had to wait for a seat to open up on a corporate jet. Within no time he was fielding calls from families with children who were cancer patients.

> "If you focus on doing something for other people, it helps one's soul recover from a huge loss."

"When you are going through the pain and suffering of losing a child, which is so unnatural," Scott said, "if you focus on doing something for other people, it helps one's soul recover from a huge loss."

Icy wanted to focus on needy children too.

"When Sargeant was sick and we were taking care of him, I was closer to God than I've ever been," Icy said. "My life became very simple. I'd wake up in the morning, and I knew what I was supposed to do. Plus, I spent a lot of time praying."

In an attempt to recapture a similar sense of purpose, Icy contacted Blythedale Children's Hospital in Valhalla, New York. It specialized in treating children with chronic, complex medical conditions, including mitochondrial diseases. The medical director at the hospital had been one of Sargent's doctors. Icy told him she wanted to volunteer at the hospital.

"Until you are in a community of sick children, you don't realize this sort of thing exists," Icy said.

She ended up being assigned to work with the youngest population, where she connected with a little boy from the Bronx. He was eighteen months old and had thick, curly hair. His condition and symptoms were nearly identical to Sargeant's. The only difference was that this boy had the ability to smile, something Sargeant was never able to do. The boy had no visitors during his long-term stay at the hospital. His family had essentially dropped him off and not returned. But Icy returned regularly. He was never able to speak to her, but he did smile.

"It was his way of letting me know he was thrilled to be with me," Icy said. "Every time this boy smiled, I felt like it was a gift from Sargeant."

The last time Icy saw the boy was right before he died. He had been transferred to an acute care unit. Icy had to pretend she was a hospital employee to gain access to the floor. When she entered the boy's room, she discovered his father at his bedside. He didn't speak English. Icy gave him a letter that explained how much his little boy had given her.

• • •

"What happens to us when we die?" It was just one of the questions Sargeant's brother asked shortly after he passed away. There were others:

"Where is Sargeant?"

"Can I talk to Sargeant?"

"Can he hear me?"

"Does he miss us too?"

The queries prompted Icy to do something she hadn't considered—write a children's book that answered those questions. The title came to her right away—*Sargeant's Heaven*—but figuring out what to say was another matter. Plus, she was raising three boys. Nevertheless, she started plugging away. A month turned into a year, and before she knew it, she had worked on the idea on and off for three years. During that time, Scott announced it was time for a family vacation. The boys were getting old enough. They decided on a ranch in Wyoming.

While there they went horseback riding. When the ranch hand saw how young the boys were, he brought out the gentlest horse in the stable. "This is Sergeant," he said. "Any of you can ride Sergeant."

Scott and Icy looked at each other. They didn't know whether to smile or cry.

Experiences like that gave Icy peace of mind. "It just seemed like he was saying, 'Everything is okay, Mom.'"

It wasn't long before she began to feel like she was supposed to have another child. She told Scott, but he was hesitant. Mitochondrial diseases were either inherited or occurred when spontaneous mutations in DNA altered the protein molecules. In Sargeant's case, experts were unable to determine which was the case. That was what had Scott anxious. What if the disease surfaced again? He couldn't bear the thought of losing another child.

Seeking guidance, Scott and Icy went to see Neely Towe, the minister at Stanwich Congregational Church in Greenwich. A graduate of Yale Divinity School, Towe had been at the family's side throughout Sargeant's illness. She welcomed Icy and Scott into her office.

> "For some people, loss diminishes them," she said. "But for you it's done the opposite. Loss has driven you to do good."

"I really, really want to have another child," Icy told her.

"That's great," Towe said.

"But he doesn't," Icy said, motioning to her husband.

Towe turned to Scott.

"I just don't know if I can get through another loss," he said.

Towe let Scott talk about his feelings before she offered some insight.

"For some people, loss diminishes them," she said. "But for you it's done the opposite. Loss has driven you to do good."

Icy went home with a deeper appreciation for her husband. Scott had suffered a lot of loss. He could easily be the kind of person that said, "Screw life. Forget God. I'm angry." But that was not what he had done.

Shortly after sitting down with Towe, Scott decided

he wanted what Icy wanted. On March 25, 2006, Icy gave birth to a baby girl. They named her Brady. When Sargeant was born, he hadn't resembled any of his older brothers. But Brady looked an awful lot like Sargeant.

"I feel he was part of choosing her," Icy said. "I can picture Sargeant saying, 'You are going to go down there, and you are going to bring some humor into the family.'"

After Brady was born, Icy determined to finish *Sargeant's Heaven*. Once she had the words down, she needed an illustrator and turned to friend Nina Weld, a local artist in Greenwich. Nina had developed juvenile rheumatoid arthritis as a child. As a result, her hands didn't look capable of holding a pencil, much less drawing pretty pictures.

"Considering the extent of my disease," Weld said, "my hands look good."

Her art looked good too. She jumped at the chance to work with Icy. "It was just an amazing thing to be able to take all this grief and everything this family went through," Weld said, "and transform it into something that would help others."

Sargeant's Heaven was self-published in 2007. Brian Williams featured it on *NBC Nightly News*, prompting over three thousand people to order copies. Icy wrote notes to everyone who purchased the book within the first six months of the on-sale date. Many of them wrote back, sharing stories about why they had bought her book. It was hard to read about other children who had died, but Icy took comfort in knowing that the book was making a difference in the lives of people who were grieving.

All proceeds were donated to organizations that help families in crisis. On one of the pages, Sargeant says good night to God at the end of a day. The illustration shows a little boy standing at a gate, facing a smiling sun. "I wanted God to be friendly and welcoming," Weld said of the illustration. "Maybe that's how I see God."

> "God puts our soul on the earth and gives us a lot of leeway to mess things up, to get into trouble, to be lucky and unlucky, to experience joy and sorrow. The world wouldn't be nearly as interesting if it was otherwise."

Scott looks at God with gratitude rather than resentment. "What a privilege to be put here on the earth," he said. "God puts our soul on the earth and gives us a lot of leeway to mess things up, to get into trouble, to be lucky and unlucky, to experience joy and sorrow. The world wouldn't be nearly as interesting if it was otherwise."

Icy still tears up on occasion when she talks about Sargeant. But thinking about him usually puts a smile on her face. "You look at things the way you want," Icy said. "We choose to see him in a better place. But what amazes me as I look at the way people handle adversity is the amount of good that can come out of it. After we lost Sargeant, we wanted his life to have significance."

I marvel at all the good Scott and Icy Frantz have accomplished. I am convinced that Sargeant is still a big part of their lives. Their story inspires those looking down the abyss of sorrow to step back from the edge and look outward instead of inward. It inspires us to find and serve someone who is hurting, someone who is lost, and, in turn, choose to make the world "a better place for those who will live in it after we are gone."

"The chance to begin again

is a compelling idea."

—BONO

CHAPTER FOUR

CHOOSE TO BELIEVE

For over thirty-seven years, Gay Byrne hosted *The Late Late Show*, the world's second-longest-running television talk show. Byrne is known as an exceptional interviewer and was the first person to introduce the Beatles on screen. He was also the first host of the popular TV series *The Meaning of Life,* where he interviewed public figures about life and its meaning. In 2013, Byrne interviewed U2's Bono, pressing the world famous rock star about whether he truly believed in Jesus Christ. Here is Bono's response: "[Jesus] went around saying he was the Messiah. That's why he was crucified. He was crucified because he said he was the Son of God. So, he either, in my view, was the Son of God or he was nuts. Forget rock-and-roll messianic complexes. I mean

Charlie Manson-type delirium. And I find it hard to accept that whole millions and millions of lives, half the earth, for 2,000 years have been touched, have felt their lives touched and inspired by some nutter. I don't believe it."

In the same interview, Bono told Byrne that he prays "to get to know the will of God, because then the prayers have more chance of coming true." In times of trouble it's tempting to choose doubt over faith. This is a story about two people in trouble—one who relied on God, and one who hoped God was real. Hope can be life-changing or, in this case, lifesaving.

> Hope can be life-changing or, in this case, lifesaving.

• • •

One of the things my wife and I enjoy most is finding restaurants in big cities that serve organic foods from local farms. But our favorite place to eat is about ten minutes from our home in rural Virginia. It's called Brix, and the dining area is so small—maybe a dozen tables at most—that there's usually just one waitress working the floor. When things get really busy, the bartender helps serve the food. The chef often comes out of the kitchen to talk with customers about the farms that source the items on the menu.

We became particularly drawn to one waitress there named Lindsay Stutsmark. She had no previous restaurant experience, but she knew how to treat people. In between bringing us appetizers and entrées, she'd talk to us about our children, our health, and our overall welfare. She became a friend, and she was part of the reason we enjoyed eating there so much. Then, one day, the owner informed us that Lindsay was on medical leave after nearly dying in a flash flood. The man who had saved her from drowning had started working part-time at the restaurant while Lindsay recovered from her injuries. My wife and I started thinking about all the times Lindsay had served us, and we decided to return the favor in a small way. We invited Lindsay and the man who'd rescued her to our home for dinner. The prayer before the meal that evening felt more meaningful. After Lindsay's near-death experience, words like *Thank you* and *Lord* took on new meaning.

> First she got swept up in an unforeseen storm. Then she hung on for dear life. Finally, when she was too beaten down to hang on any longer, her faith got her through.

In all our previous restaurant conversations with Lindsay, she had never brought up God or faith. But much of the dinner table conversation at our home that night revolved around Lindsay's struggle to survive. In that context, she had a lot to say about faith. So did the man who'd rescued her. At one point during the storm, Lindsay was too fatigued to hold on, but her rescuer kept yelling, "Don't let go of the tree."

And she'd felt a strength beyond her own holding her in place until rescue workers arrived.

I saw a powerful metaphor for life in Lindsay's experience. First she got swept up in an unforeseen storm. Then she hung on for dear life. Finally, when she was too beaten down to hang on any longer, her faith got her through.

That night over dinner I asked the two if they'd mind sharing their experiences with me for this book.

• • •

Lindsay Stutsmark felt like her life was headed nowhere. But she didn't know what to do about it. At forty-one, she was waiting tables at a small restaurant in rural Virginia, not far from the Appalachian Trail. She used to be a schoolteacher in North Carolina, helping disadvantaged children learn to read and write. Teaching was the one thing that had given her a sense of purpose and fulfillment. But a variety of factors—stress, anxiety, and self-doubt—had led her to walk away from her passion a few years earlier. Since then she'd been taking drink orders and serving lamb ragout, braised leeks, and dry-rubbed hanger steaks with vanilla bourbon pan sauce to a mixed clientele of college professors, business professionals, and lawyers. She made just enough in tips to cover the rent on her one-bedroom cottage, where she lived alone. It was getting harder and harder to get out of bed in the morning.

On May 13, 2012, she got called in to work the

lunch shift. Hiking season was underway, and the restaurant was offering a two-for-one special for hikers. Ben Glass, thirty-seven, had set out to hike from one end of the Appalachian Trail to the other. He and his dog, Max, had started in Georgia weeks earlier. The plan was to get to Maine by the end of summer. Ben had plenty of time. He worked as a roofer in Louisiana, where he'd saved up enough money to take the summer off. A buddy had agreed to go along.

But while making their way through the Blue Ridge Mountains, Ben's buddy had fallen and injured his leg. He needed medical attention and a few days' worth of rest before resuming. And so they'd ventured off the trail near Lexington, Virginia. After finding a hotel, Ben took his dog into town in search of a place to eat. A sidewalk sign advertising a hiker's special drew him to the restaurant where Lindsay worked.

The moment she saw him—short, stocky build; hair in a ponytail; beard; cargo shorts; and boots—she figured he had just come off the trail. She seated him and took his order—two steaks, one for him and one for his dog, who was waiting outside. When the order was up, Lindsay took the food to Max and served him as if he were a person. Max liked that. So did Ben.

The lunch crowd was thin that day. Ben hung around. Lindsay kept refilling his water glass. By the time her shift ended, she'd learned that Ben was sticking around for a few days while his friend rested his leg. She was off the following day. She offered to pick him and Max up and take them out to her place.

. . .

Lindsay lived alongside a river. A short, narrow bridge connected her dirt driveway to the main road. At the right time of day, she could see the fish as the water flowed past. The nearest store was twelve miles away. Lindsay promised she'd take Ben shopping for supplies and dog food. Besides, she needed groceries too.

Ben was in no rush. He appreciated having someone to talk to. While Lindsay whipped up some lunch, he wasted no time getting to his favorite topic: Christianity.

Lindsay didn't expect religion to come up. Ben was a roofer and an outdoorsman, a guy who had taken off three months to hike the Appalachian Trail. He didn't strike her as the type to spend a lot of time in church.

Ben admitted he didn't belong to a particular congregation, but he was a big believer in Christianity. He didn't come across as self-righteous or pious. The Golden Rule was more his

> Ben was a big believer in Christianity. He didn't come across as self-righteous or pious. The Golden Rule was more his speed—"Do unto others as you would have them do unto you."

speed—"Do unto others as you would have them do unto you."

He hadn't always been this way, he admitted. As a teenager he'd gotten into a lot of trouble. He became a devoted Christian at age twenty. He had spent most of his adult years trying to help people in need. It was his way of giving back. After Hurricane Katrina, for example, he went door-to-door helping people who had incurred property damage.

Ben seemed so certain of his convictions. Lindsay wasn't so sure of hers. She believed in God but not enough to stand up and declare it. Not enough to call herself a Christian. She didn't tell Ben that, though. She wasn't sure how he'd react.

"Enough about me," Ben said as they visited. "What did you do before you were a waitress?"

"Teach," she said.

Ben was surprised.

Lindsay explained that she'd worked at a middle school for troubled children in North Carolina. The students had come from underprivileged backgrounds. It had been extremely rewarding but also emotionally draining. After a while, she'd left the school and returned to Virginia, where she'd become a substitute teacher in the public school system.

Ben found her teaching background interesting. He had grown up in a housing project in Louisiana—the only white kid in his neighborhood. The only white student in his school. He related to some of the situations Lindsay re-counted. They ended up talking for hours.

Lindsay couldn't remember the last time she'd had such heartfelt conversation. She barely knew this guy. Yet she had spent an entire day talking with him. There was something different about him. He was so unpretentious it was easy to let her guard down.

She went to her bedroom and retrieved a photo album. It contained pictures of all the children she had taught in North Carolina. She told Ben something about each child.

"I just have one question," he said.

"What's that?"

"Why are you waiting tables instead of teaching children?"

She closed the album. "You know, that's a really good question."

• • •

It was after five when they finally headed to the store to pick up camping supplies and groceries at the Dollar General. They were checking out when the cashier said, "You two be careful out there. Supposed to be a really bad storm coming."

The road back to Lindsay's place ran along the river. Ben offered to drive. They'd gone less than two miles when the sky darkened, and the rain came down so hard it sounded like rocks on the roof. Within minutes the river was on the verge of cresting its banks. Lindsay's place was still ten miles away. Nervous, she suggested they turn back. A coworker of hers lived by the store, she said. They could stay there until the storm passed.

Ben pointed out that his dog was at Lindsay's place. He wouldn't do well all alone in a strange house during a bad storm.

And so they kept driving, eventually reaching the first of two bridges they needed to cross. It was under about a foot of water.

Lindsay panicked. "We'll never make it."

Ben gunned it. Water shot from beneath the car and the engine sputtered, but they made it. Farther down the road they reached the small bridge that was part of the driveway leading to Lindsay's house. It was under water too. The current was so strong it shifted the front end of the car as they approached.

Lindsay screamed, "Back up!"

Ben fumbled to shift the gears.

"Reverse!" she shouted. "Reverse!"

He lurched the vehicle back from the bridge. Lindsay's house was less than a hundred yards away, but they couldn't even see it. It was only six-thirty, but it was as dark as midnight, the rain coming down in sheets.

They drove up the main road to Lindsay's nearest neighbor, Rodney Swisher. He was a firefighter and owned a four-wheel-drive Ford Bronco. They loaded the groceries into

Rodney's vehicle, and he drove them to the bridge. But he stopped when he saw fallen trees—roots and all—flowing past them. The bridge was barely the length of a few cars. Still, there was too much debris flowing over it to risk driving on it.

Lindsay desperately wanted to get home. Ben thought they could get across on foot. Lindsay turned to Rodney for his opinion. "What do you think?"

"It looks pretty bad," he said. "But if you do it, stay to the left."

"C'mon," Ben said. "Let's try."

Lindsay looked at Rodney. "Don't leave until you see us on the other side."

"I won't."

"And leave your headlights on."

"I will."

Ben put a couple bags of groceries under each arm and stepped onto the bridge. Lindsay grabbed the other two bags and followed. They were instantly in water up to their thighs, and the current was so strong it sucked the bags from their hands. In seconds the groceries had vanished downstream.

Lindsay started screaming.

"Get behind me!" Ben shouted.

"I can't do this!" she cried, panicked.

He grabbed her hand. "I got you! I got you!"

Lindsay took one more step, and the current swept her

off her feet, instantly breaking Ben's grip and plunging her underwater. Fully submerged, she flailed as her body headed downstream. Spinning uncontrollably, she gulped water as she tried to scream for help. There was nothing she could do.

Suddenly her head was jerked out of the water. Ben had jumped in the rushing river and grabbed the hood of her sweatshirt. She started vomiting up muddy water and gasping for air. He held on to her as the current slammed him into a large, partly submerged tree near the riverbank. Still clutching the hood, he wrapped his other arm and his legs around the trunk of the tree.

"Grab the tree!" Ben shouted.

Lindsay didn't respond.

"Grab it! Now!"

Mustering all the strength she had, she wrapped her arms around it. The water was up to her chest, but the tree was sheltering her from the current, and she could breathe. Ben, on the other hand, had his back to the current. Dead animals, logs, and debris pummeled his back.

"We have to get up this tree," he said.

"I can't," Lindsay protested.

"We have to."

There was no way. Lindsay had experienced anxiety and fear at different times in her life, but nothing compared to the sheer terror of what she faced now. She wasn't letting go of the tree. She wasn't going anywhere.

"Don't let go of the tree!" he shouted.

Fearful he'd get knocked out and drown if he stayed put, Ben shimmied up the tree. When he got high enough, he removed his shirt and tied it to a limb. On the opposite side of the river, Rodney was sure Lindsay and Ben had drowned. He had just climbed into his Bronco when his high beams picked up the reflection from Ben's shirt. Next he spotted Ben. He shouted for him to hang on. Help was on the way.

> Nothing compared to the sheer terror of what she faced now. She wasn't letting go of the tree. She wasn't going anywhere.

The rain kept coming. Three hours passed. Lindsay hadn't moved.

"I just can't hold on anymore."

"You have to," Ben said.

"Why aren't they coming?"

"They'll be here."

"I'm so tired."

"Don't let go!"

Freezing and exhausted, she figured she was going to die. Memories of the past ran through her mind. Mistakes. Regrets. Sins.

Crying, she wished she could go back. If only she could make things right. She pleaded with God. Rather than praying to be saved from the flood, she begged for forgiveness. She wanted to die with a clear conscience.

"Don't let go!" Ben said.

"I can't do this anymore." Lindsay was giving up.

"If you let go, you have to face our Lord," Ben said, trying to motivate her.

Lindsay said nothing.

"Are you ready to face him?" he asked.

> She pleaded with God. Rather than praying to be saved from the flood, she begged for forgiveness. She wanted to die with a clear conscience.

Despondent, Lindsay saw her deceased grandparents. It seemed as if they were yelling to her: *You can't let go. You can't let go!*

"You can't let go!" Ben also shouted.

No longer capable of mustering the strength to hang on, she prayed, "If this is my time, I'm ready. If it isn't, give me the strength to know what I need to do."

• • •

Abraham Lincoln nearly drowned in a creek as a child. Historian Stephen Oates tells the story of the former president being saved by a boy who waded into the water and pulled him out. Lincoln's mother, Nancy, believed her son didn't drown that day because it wasn't his time. God had "other designs," she said. And she taught her son the Baptist creed of fatalism that said, "Nothing can hinder the execution of the designs of Providence. What is to be will be and we can do nothing about it."

In Lincoln's case, the course of human history changed

because someone chose to go into the water and pull him out. In this case, the course of Lindsay's life took a dramatic turn when Ben refused to give up on her. For the next hour she was in and out of consciousness. Ben kept talking to her, but all she did was moan periodically. At one a.m., a Swift Water Rescue team arrived in a boat. Medics hovered above the scene in a helicopter. By then Lindsay and Ben had been stranded for more than six hours. When rescuers reached Lindsay, they couldn't pry her limbs from the tree. She had held on so tightly the bark was imbedded in her legs. The tree was literally holding her.

It took rescue workers nearly an hour to separate her limbs from the trunk. She was in shock by the time they put her in the boat.

"I just want to go home," she cried.

"Sorry, ma'am, you are not going to be able to go home. We have to put you in a helicopter."

Overcome with hypothermia, her body shut down. Aboard the chopper, medics cut off her waterlogged clothing. Her skin was blue; her heart rate was fading. They wrapped her in blankets.

She regained consciousness at the hospital. When she was asked for her religious preference, she said, "If I didn't die in the water, I will not die in this hospital."

• • •

Lindsay was released the following day. She had lost the hearing in her right ear. There was damage to the nerve endings in her legs, and the muscles in her legs were deeply bruised. And she had plenty of lacerations. The doctors said she'd need to spend the next week or two on bed rest. Scarring would likely be significant.

She didn't mind. She was alive. The scars would be a constant reminder that God was real.

"I prayed to God for help," she said. "I had control over letting go, so I didn't let go. But He gave me strength I didn't have."

> "I prayed to God for help," she said. "I had control over letting go, so I didn't let go. But He gave me strength I didn't have."

It was a month before Lindsay felt well enough to return to work. Ben cared for her while she recuperated, cooking her meals and keeping her company. Eventually she returned to the restaurant, and he returned to the trail. But life got harder before it got easier. Her legs hadn't fully healed, making waitressing difficult. The nerves in her legs produced sharp pains, and her muscles constantly ached. She regained some of her hearing, but she had regular panic attacks and suffered from insomnia. And she was petrified of water. Even showers and baths caused fear. She started seeing a counselor to help her deal with the anxiety. She prayed a lot, too.

Eleven months after nearly drowning, Lindsay left waitressing and returned to teach at a school for kids with autism. It was a big first step. A few months later she accepted a position at a public high school working with special-needs students. Her legs still hurt. She struggled to sleep. And she was still terrified of water. But she kept telling herself, *Lindsay, you have to realize that for you to have survived, there is a reason for your existence. God has put you here for a bigger reason than you know. Instead of being scared and having all this anxiety, you have to start living again. You can't be afraid.*

"I used to be one of those people who was afraid to say, 'Yes, I believe in God,'" Lindsay said. "Until that night in the river, I never felt His presence. But now I know there is a reason for my existence. That's what got me back into helping children."

> "God has put you here for a bigger reason than you know. Instead of being scared and having all this anxiety, you have to start living again. You can't be afraid."

After hiking the Appalachian Trail, Ben returned to Virginia and took a job at the restaurant where Lindsay used to work. He and Lindsay remain close friends. She credits him with helping her find happiness. And she credits God for giving her a new life and a new purpose. Lindsay chose to believe what Ben already believed—that God had a plan for her.

I began this chapter with words from Bono. I'll close

with an excerpt from an essay he titled "Do You Know Where Your Soul Is?" In it, Bono wrote, "Of all the Christian festivals, it is the Easter parade that demands the most faith—pushing you past reverence for creation, through bewilderment at the idea of a virgin birth, and into the far-fetched and far-reaching idea that death is not the end. The cross as crossroads. Whatever your religious or nonreligious views, the chance to begin again is a compelling idea."

"Everyone has noticed how hard it is to turn our thoughts to God when everything is going well with us. We 'have all we want' is a terrible saying when 'all' does not include God."

—C. S. LEWIS

CHAPTER FIVE

CHOOSE TO PRAY

"You can't see anything properly while your eyes are blurred with tears." C. S. Lewis wrote those words while grieving the death of his wife, Joy. He described that period of his life as a "time when there is nothing at all in your soul except a cry for help." This dark time prompted him to write *A Grief Observed*, a sad, honest account of what happens to a man of faith whose world goes dark. Lewis experienced doubt and resentment and despair during this period. But he never stopped praying. He wrote, "Everyone has noticed how hard it is to turn our thoughts to God when everything is going well with us. We 'have all we want' is a terrible saying when 'all' does not include God. As St. Augustine says somewhere, 'God wants to give us something, but cannot, because our hands are full—there's nowhere for Him to put it.' Or, as a friend of mine said, 'We regard God as an airman regards his parachute; it's there for emergencies but he hopes he'll never have to use it.'"

This is a story about two people brought together by desperate circumstances and the power of prayer.

• • •

In 2000, my literary agent told me that a woman who wanted to hire me as a consultant had contacted him. She indicated that an Indian tribe had sued the private school her son attended, claiming the school had been built on tribal land. The tribe wanted the land back so they could construct a casino. I was fresh out of law school and had just published *Without Reservation*, a book about a counterfeit Indian tribe that sued private landowners, then annexed the land and built the world's largest casino on it. The woman who called my agent had read my book and hoped that I would help the private school.

"What do you think?" I asked my agent.

"I think you should call her," he said.

The woman's name was Judith Paixao. She lived just outside New York City. When I reached her she asked if she and her husband could take me out to dinner. I was living in Boston at the time. They offered to come to me. And they encouraged me to bring my wife and children. Over dinner I made two observations: when our newborn cried, Judith walked him around the restaurant for a lengthy period of time, enabling my wife to enjoy her meal; and Judith and her husband wore expensive clothes and insisted on paying for our dinner. I concluded that she was very considerate of others and very well-off.

I ended up working for the private school. A year later Judith worked for my campaign when I ran for U.S. Congress in Connecticut. Judith was a woman who seemed like she had an idyllic life. Then hard things started happening. Her husband was diagnosed with cancer, and his final years were miserable. Then he died and left Judith both lonely and in deep financial trouble. One weekend she was visiting our family, and I invited her to attend church with us. That's when I discovered she was a person of deep faith and conviction. Her faith in God was the anchor that had gotten her through some painful changes and circumstances. Eventually I asked if she'd mind me including her in a book about finding peace amidst turmoil. She said she'd be honored. I'm glad I took my agent's advice and called her back. This is her story.

> Her faith in God was the anchor that had gotten her through some painful changes and circumstances.

• • •

On September 3, 2005, Judith Paixao, forty-nine, sat in a chair inside her artistically renovated barn home, her eyes on the Weather Channel. A few feet away, her husband Arthur, seventy-three, lay in bed, racked with pain and heavily medicated with cancer drugs and prescription pain pills. The live-in hospice nurse was in and out. It was midday. Sunlight streamed through the windows as images of Hurricane Katrina battering New Orleans flashed across the television screen. Judith put her hand over her mouth. She had been born in Baton Rouge and had lived in New Orleans for years. She had family there. A correspondent reported that over eighty percent of the city was underwater. Hundreds of thousands of people were homeless. The death toll was mounting.

"Arthur, New Orleans is ravaged," Judith said.

He ignored her.

"It's underwater," she continued. "Those poor people."

"Who the hell cares?" he snapped. "I'm dying!"

She looked at him and bit her tongue. It had been three years since she had walked away from her thriving career as a jewelry designer to care for Arthur full-time. By mid-2005 he lacked the strength to leave the house. He'd been bedridden for months. Miserable and bitter, he often treated Judith with contempt. She kept telling herself that he wasn't himself, that he didn't mean it, that the chemotherapy and other drugs were a factor. Still, she felt like a punching bag.

As soon as he nodded off, she went outside for some

fresh air. Her daily walks through their wooded estate in rural Connecticut provided her only means of escape. No one understood her situation. She had no one to tell. Finding herself alone, she sat on a stone patio next to the pond, her feet dangling in the water. Terrified of spending the rest of her life alone, she buried her face in her hands. She used to be so vibrant.

Back in 1978, Judith had started a real estate marketing firm, performing feasibility studies and consulting for commercial developers. She was twenty-five. At the time, Arthur was an accomplished architect and one of the biggest waterfront developers on the East Coast. In the early eighties, he hired Judith to be the project director for an historic district he was developing in Norwalk, Connecticut. A decade later they became business partners. By then Judith was divorced and raising a young son, Benjamin. He was three weeks old the first time she took him sailing. She'd strapped his infant racecar bed to the mast and spent a month in the waters off the shores of Rhode Island. As a single mother overseeing big waterfront developments, she raised her son to believe that he could do anything.

In the mid-nineties, Arthur and Judith formed a real estate development partnership and were chosen to redevelop part of the waterfront in Knoxville, Tennessee. Judith moved there as the partner in charge, living on the water with Benjamin. While there, Benjamin turned eleven. Using money he had saved while working as a marina dockhand, he purchased a small fishing boat, a Boston Whaler. It was used, but it was his. He was a boy with big dreams, and his mother encouraged him to pursue them.

At the conclusion of the Knoxville project, Judith was at the height of her career. With money to burn, she went on a clothes-shopping spree one day. Unable to find suitable matching jewelry, she set out to make some of her own. The owner of an upscale dress boutique liked her pieces so much that she requested permission to sell them. Within a year Judith had over a hundred customers. Six months later she walked away from real estate development to pursue her passion for designing and making jewelry.

Before long she was designing pieces for the head of marketing at H. Stern in New York City. By that time, Arthur had left his wife of many years. He and Judith found a home and moved in together. She was in her early forties. He was in his mid-sixties. Their differences went beyond age. He liked his red meat rare and his whiskey neat. She ate organic vegetables and drank smoothies. He liked hockey. She preferred museums. He read the *Journal*; she read the *Times*.

But they both loved to sail. And Arthur had told more than one friend that he had never loved anyone like he loved Judith. Benjamin was just finishing middle school when Judith moved in with Arthur. That year Arthur was diagnosed with cancer. Initially his medical situation was manageable. But the fallout from leaving a longstanding relationship to start a new one was messy. Arthur's adult children resented Judith. And Arthur was constantly critical of Benjamin, shaking the boy's confidence. Judith considered leaving. But as Arthur's cancer progressed, she felt obligated to stay. He often said that she was his reason for living.

Yet Judith knew it was debilitating for Benjamin to live under the same roof with Arthur, so she enrolled him in a private boarding school, refusing to let Arthur pay for any of the tuition. She cobbled together the money from her jewelry business. Then, when Arthur's cancer approached the advanced stage, Judith finally married him. It seemed like the honorable thing to do at the time. Still, it was detrimental to her relationship with her son. So many times she wished she could go back to the days of being a single mother sailing with her baby boy, but she couldn't undo her choice. *It's my cross to bear*, she'd tell herself.

• • •

As Judith finished her reprieve at the pond, she wiped her eyes, then headed back inside. Arthur was still asleep. She didn't bother trying to wake him. Later that night he passed away. She never really got to say good-bye. After ten years, his last words to her were *Who the hell cares? I'm dying!*

• • •

Following the funeral, Judith drove to the marina where Arthur kept their forty-eight-foot sailboat, *Shillelagh*. He had left it to her in his will. Numb, she climbed aboard and walked to the bow. She had never experienced losing a loved one. If only she had a shoulder to cry on. But Arthur's family had shunned her. She couldn't burden Benjamin; he was too young and had been wounded by Arthur. At fifty-three she was alone, afraid, and scared. What would happen to her? Who was she now? Where did she go from here? How did she rediscover herself?

> At fifty-three she was alone, afraid, and scared. What would happen to her? Who was she now? Where did she go from here? How did she rediscover herself?

The answers, she believed, lay at sea. She and Arthur had lived aboard a boat in St. Petersburg, Florida, while he underwent a round of cancer treatments. She figured she'd sail there. The journey would take at least two weeks. That would give her plenty of time to think, pray, and ponder.

That afternoon she telephoned a captain who was a friend of her late husband. She asked if she could hire him to sail with her to St. Petersburg. The captain was willing, but after looking the boat over, he determined it wasn't seaworthy for such a long journey. It needed a lot of work. He said to call him back when the boat was ready.

Judith struggled to find help. Two months later the boat still wasn't ready. The captain called and told her he was no longer available. He had accepted a last-minute invitation to sail for another client.

Judith asked him to reconsider.

He couldn't. He was sailing to Europe.

"Look," the captain told her. "I have a really good friend who is a great sailor. Maybe he'll help you."

"Who is he?"

"He's a cinematographer. He shoots commercials for Victoria's Secret, but when he's not working, he does one or two adventure sails a year. He knows what he's doing."

Judith didn't see how a man who filmed lingerie commercials could get her and her sailboat down the Atlantic coast.

"He's in between shoots now," the captain continued. "So this is a good time."

Desperate, she asked what it would cost her.

"He doesn't do it for hire," the captain said. "He just loves sailing. Do you want me to call him?"

• • •

Kev Lombard was paid a lot of money to look at beautiful women through his lens. As a fashion photographer for Victoria's Secret, he'd worked with many of the company's top models. Heidi Klum. Tyra Banks. Naomi Campbell. He'd also done work for Ralph Lauren, Tommy Hilfiger, and other big names. Men liked to joke that he had the best job in the world.

Kev didn't see it that way. The money was great, but his sense of fulfillment was low. Filming big runway fashion shows and fashion videos was superficial. At fifty-four he longed to do something purposeful. He thought about going back to making documentaries or children's films, something that had earned him three Emmy Awards earlier in his career. But first he had to sort out his personal life.

Estranged from his wife, Kev had become reclusive. His Connecticut home was virtually empty, and he seldom stayed there. Whenever he wasn't shooting on location, he'd head off to Deltaville, Virginia, where he had a twenty-eight-foot sailboat. Alone, he'd work on it in hopes of one day making a solo trip around the world. Spiritually, he longed for something more. Whatever it was, he hoped he'd find it at sea.

> His purpose in life, he believed, was to help people.

A lifelong Catholic, Kev believed in God, but he hadn't been to church in years. He'd been exploring Buddhism. More than anything, he was searching. His purpose in life, he believed, was to help people. When his friend the boat captain called and said he knew a woman who needed help sailing a boat to Florida, Kev was interested.

"I think she's in her eighties," the captain told him. The only other descriptor he offered was her hair color—silver. He also mentioned that her husband had recently died of cancer.

That definitely sounded like someone in need of help.

Kev took down her name, along with the location of the boat.

On November 10, 2005, Judith went to the boat early to work on the furniture below deck. The temperature was in the forties. She was removing the coverings on a new set of pillows and listening to the *Lion King* soundtrack when she heard someone knock on the hull. She looked up to see a well-built man in deck shoes and a Barbour jacket. His head was shaved and he had a tan.

"Can I help you?"

"My name is Kev Lombard. I am looking for Judith."

"I'm Judith."

Kev hesitated. She had silver hair, but it was stylish and rich. And there was no way this woman was in her eighties. She looked his age, maybe even younger. As a fashion photographer he couldn't help noticing her fine jewelry. He'd expected none of this.

Judith was puzzled too. This guy didn't fit her stereotype for a man who made lingerie commercials. Pillow in hand, she smiled and invited him aboard. They talked. She showed him around. He asked about the boat. She asked about his availability. An hour later, they were still talking and she was still holding the pillow. "Look," he said, "if we're going out on the ocean, there are things more important than upholstery."

It was the first time she had laughed in months.

Judith spent three weeks helping Kev prepare the boat.

The Sunday after Thanksgiving 2005, they set sail. A captain's mate joined them. The plan was to go from New York Harbor to St. Petersburg in ten days. En route, Judith planned on doing a lot of thinking. Kev was looking forward to some time away to clear his mind too.

The winter air coming off the water was frigid, but Judith felt unleashed. Within hours of sailing past the Statue of Liberty, they could see nothing but ocean in every direction. It felt like they were in the middle of nowhere. The sun was setting. Kev was at the helm. His mate was resting below deck. Dressed in four layers of thermal underwear, Judith went to the front of the boat to think and pray.

Raised Episcopalian, she had always been a person of deep faith. But while living with Arthur, she had gotten out of the habit of regularly going to church. It had been so long since she'd had a spiritual conversation with God (or anyone else) that she no longer knew what she believed. Staring at the horizon, she wanted to pray, but no words came to mind. Silent and still, she took in the view. At least it was peaceful.

It didn't take long before she was freezing. After going below deck to warm up, she emerged with supper: grilled cheese sandwiches and cups of coffee. Kev wrapped both hands around the steaming mug she offered him and sipped. Neither of them was very good at small talk. Judith went right to what was on her mind—the newly renovated home on the estate she had inherited. It felt like an albatross.

Kev didn't understand. The architecture and the setting sounded amazing. What was the problem?

She explained that right after Arthur died, she discovered that he had placed a number of mortgages on the estate. The combined monthly payment was $28,000, not including taxes and utilities.

Kev raised his eyebrows.

Embarrassed, Judith said there was no way she could sustain that. She had inherited some money, but she was an unemployed jewelry designer. More to the point, the outsized mortgage was proof that she and her husband had been living far beyond their means. The property represented an empty lifestyle she wanted to leave behind.

To a certain extent, Kev could relate. He had been an award-winning director and a cameraman for *Reading Rainbow* and *Sesame Street*. He'd worked in network television, shooting for *60 Minutes* and *20/20*. At one time he'd even been Walter Cronkite's personal cinematographer and spent a month with him in Egypt. By the time Kev became a director and producer of fashion-industry television commercials, he'd reached the zenith of his career. But the work felt shallow. He longed for something else.

What, though? He was unsure. His life felt a bit like his career—it lacked a sense of purpose. One of the reasons he'd agreed to help Judith sail to Florida was to give himself the time and space he needed to figure out the next phase of his life. It reassured him to realize that Judith was going through a midlife crisis of her own. They ended up talking until dawn.

The following night, shortly after supper, it started snowing. Soon hailstones pelted the deck. Without warning, twenty-foot swells started slamming the boat. Wind gusts topped forty knots. They were more than a hundred miles off shore. It was immediately clear they were in grave danger. Their only option was to try to navigate through the storm.

Silently, Judith prayed. This time the words came easily. *Oh, dear God, help us! Please.*

> Their only option was to try to navigate through the storm. Silently, Judith prayed. This time the words came easily. *Oh, dear God, help us! Please.*

For the next eight hours they battled the elements. The storm didn't let up until dawn. By then they were exhausted and the boat had taken on a lot of water. With some investigation, Kev figured out that one of the boat's main pumps had failed and that the bottom of the boat was full of bilge— black water that had been spit into the boat instead of pumped out to sea. Luckily Kev had brought along a spare pump. He spent much of the third day siphoning the black water from the boat.

Rough seas accompanied them all the way to North Carolina, where they encountered another violent storm off the shore of Cape Hatteras. It hit after midnight. Judith was asleep on the floor in the main salon, wedged between the settee and the captain's table. Kev had the night watch. The boat was on autopilot. As soon as heavy seas starting tossing the boat, Kev realized the boat was taking on water again. He had to find the source.

He told his ship's mate to take the helm while he headed below deck with a flashlight. Judith sat up when she saw Kev peering through the floorboards. Suddenly a wave hit, dislodging a heavy wooden seat and sending it flying across the cabin. It struck Kev in the head.

"Kev!" Judith screamed.

Stunned, he dropped his light and glanced up at Judith.

She rose to go toward him just as another wave hit, knocking her off her feet and propelling her across the wet floor on her belly toward Kev. He locked arms with her just before she hit the wall. Face-to-face, they looked into each other's eyes and started laughing. The boat was at risk of sinking. They were in a life-and-death situation. Yet they were laughing and holding on to each other.

She looked at his head. He wasn't bleeding, but a lump was forming.

"I can't keep the boat on autopilot," he said. "I'm going to have to steer us through the storm."

"What do you need me to do?"

"Call out the oncoming squalls. You're going to have to yell loud."

She bundled up.

"You can do this!" he said. "You'll be fine."

She should have been frightened, but Kev was so confident she didn't panic.

Under her breath she begged God for their safety. The squalls were so violent that capsizing was a real likelihood, dying at sea a distinct possibility.

Kev didn't let on, but he was worried. The storm was as bad as anything he had ever experienced. The winds exceeded forty knots. Suddenly the forward butterfly hatch was hit by a wave and came off, and they started taking on more water. Judith took the helm while Kev and the ship's mate worked on securing the hatch. She clung to the wheel, acutely aware that her life was in the hands of a man she barely knew. Yet she trusted him completely.

> She clung to the wheel, acutely aware that her life was in the hands of a man she barely knew.

By the time Kev returned to the helm, his lips were quivering from the cold, and he was shaking from being drenched by freezing seawater. The bump on his head had swelled to the size of an egg, but the hatch was secure.

• • •

It felt like morning would never come. But it did. The boat was damaged. They were soaked, cold, and fatigued. But they were alive. And sunrise never looked so good.

"Why do most storms always seem to come in the dead of night?" Judith said.

Kev smiled. It did seem that way.

They celebrated their survival with a freeze-dried meal, some granola bars, and a pot of coffee. When they said grace they held hands and thanked God they were alive. Judith prayed with her eyes wide open as she faced Kev. He met her glance. It had been so long since he'd held a woman's hand. She couldn't remember the last time she'd prayed aloud.

After the meal, they confronted what to do about the boat. The back-to-back storms had damaged it to the point that it wasn't safe to keep sailing. Kev was capable of making the repairs, but he had to get to a port.

Just north of Cape Fear, they docked at a marina for nearly three days. There was no way they were going to make it to St. Petersburg in time for Kev to get to Los Angeles for the fashion shoot he'd scheduled with Chico's. They decided to go as far as Ft. Lauderdale and call it quits.

On their final night at sea, they never went to sleep. Under a starry sky, they talked about everything from jewelry and photography to art and spirituality. They were both sleep deprived, but neither of them wanted morning to come. When they reached port, they rented a car and rushed to the airport. It was a quiet ride. For ten days they had worked side by side in the most adverse conditions. Fighting to stay alive was the most exhilarating thing either of them had experienced. Judith had never trusted someone so completely, or been trusted so completely. Her eyes welled with tears.

> Judith had never trusted someone so completely, or been trusted so completely.

At the curb Kev slung his bag over his shoulder and hugged Judith. Everything that could go wrong on the trip had gone wrong. The storms had left no time for peaceful contemplation, no opportunity for searching. But in the midst of the struggle he had found a soul mate.

• • •

Judith left her boat in Florida and flew home to Connecticut. As soon as Kev finished his shoot in LA, he boarded a plane and met up with her. They spent Christmas Eve together. Over the next year, they were inseparable.

In 2007, Judith and Kev were married and made wholesale lifestyle changes. He quit making commercials for the fashion industry. She sold the sailboat and the estate. They reduced their possessions to what they could pack into a storage unit and purchased a new sailboat that became their home.

In hopes of doing something to express their gratitude, they started a foundation to help wounded Marines. Their objective was to help train soldiers and sailors—many of whom had returned from Iraq and Afghanistan with serious physical injuries and post-traumatic stress disorder—for second careers in the television and film industries.

"We got rid of all of the material things," Judith said. "We lived on a sailboat and dedicated our time and talents to helping those who had been wounded while serving our country. It was our way of giving back."

Judith administered the school, and Kev taught the wounded Marines. In a four-year period they served almost one hundred veterans. One was a Marine scout sniper who had served multiple tours in Iraq. An explosive device detonated by insurgents had hit his Humvee. The sniper was hurled from the vehicle, sustaining brain and spinal trauma. Yet he managed to crawl 130 meters on his belly to save other soldiers who were in harm's way. For that he received the Purple Heart. After returning to the States, he was walking home from a convenience store one evening in the San Francisco area when a motorist randomly shot him four times, leaving him to die in the street. Miraculously, he survived after undergoing emergency surgery. The shooter was never found. Judith and Kev prayed with and for this Marine sniper and his family many, many times. They worked with him, too. He eventually found a job as a film editor.

"Working with these men profoundly changed our lives," Judith said. "It also drew us closer to God and turned our focus away from ourselves and channeled it toward others—soldiers and their families—who have been asked to shoulder such a huge burden by our country."

In 2012, Judith and Kev downsized again when they were offered a chance to be artists in residence in Bermuda. They purchased a modest sailboat and headed for the island.

"When we sailed together the first time, we were sailing away from our problems," Judith said. "This time we were sailing toward our future."

Bermuda is known for its sea glass. Kev taught film and projection classes and had his students help him produce a documentary on the history of sea glass in Bermuda. Judith taught students how to make jewelry from the glass. Financially, they made just enough to get by. They even joined an Anglican congregation. Spiritually they felt reborn.

> "When we sailed together the first time, we were sailing away from our problems," Judith said. "This time we were sailing toward our future."

"The bottles and sea glass of Bermuda are like a metaphor for life," Kev said. "We start out whole and beautiful and with a purpose. But we are delicate and fragile. Somewhere along the line we might become broken and discarded. Then life has a way of throwing us into the journey, tumbling us in the tides, and over time polishing us until we become like precious jewels."

Kev and Judith had gone on a journey to find answers. They'd ended up finding each other. For the first time in a long time, they also felt more grounded spiritually. It took a violent storm to bring them to that place.

"It was all prayer," Judith said. "That's what made the difference. No question about it. After the trip we started praying regularly. And we just continually say thanks for still being alive."

I'm as guilty as the next guy when it comes to behaving like the airman C. S. Lewis described—regarding God like a parachute for emergencies only. Judith and Kev have reminded me of the value of praying regularly, especially in good times. One of the keys to living an abundant life is staying connected with and expressing gratitude to Him who gives life.

> "It was all prayer," Judith said. "That's what made the difference. No question about it."

"It scared him to be different.

He couldn't understand

why he had come into the

world without a voice."

—E. B. WHITE

CHAPTER SIX

Choose to Be Strong

One of my all-time favorite books is E. B. White's *The Trumpet of the Swan.* It's the story of two trumpeter swans—a cob and his wife—who give birth to five cygnets. The youngest of the five—a swan named Louis—can't speak. This produces anxiety and sadness as Louis tries to interact with other young swans. For one thing, Louis is unable to find a mate due to his inability to call out to a female swan. In an attempt to encourage Louis, his father tells him:

> Do not let unnatural sadness settle over you, Louis. Swans must be cheerful, not sad; graceful, not awkward; brave, not cowardly. Remember that the world is full of youngsters who have some sort of handicap that they must overcome. You apparently

have a speech defect. I am sure you will overcome it, in time. There may even be some slight advantage, at your age, in not being able to say anything. It compels you to be a good listener.

The cob also made his son a promise that one day he would make it possible for Louis to use his voice. He told him that there was a mechanical device called a trumpet. And although the cob had never heard of an instance where a trumpeter swan needed a trumpet, he felt Louis was a unique case, and he promised to one day obtain a trumpet for his son.

White wrote this about Louis: "He felt frightened at being different from his brothers and sisters. It scared him to be different. He couldn't understand why he had come into the world without a voice. Everyone else seemed to have a voice. Why didn't he? . . . Then he remembered that his father had promised to help, and he felt better."

It's amazing what a child can do when a parent promises to help.

This next story is about a boy who came into the world with a different voice. And it's a story about a mother who promised to help him. It's a story about choosing to be strong.

• • •

When I started writing this book, my editor told me I should really consider talking to his sister. She would be an ideal candidate, he said, for inclusion in a book about choosing to be happy even when life beats you down. Her nine-year-old boy had undergone just over ninety surgeries, my editor told me. That amounted to nearly ten surgeries per year. I had a hard time fathoming it. Then my editor said there was more. His sister's husband had been diagnosed with cancer, and their house had been destroyed in a tornado. At one point she had texted her brother and said, "How strong does God think I am?"

Her story stands out as perhaps the most extraordinary in terms of demonstrating an undying willingness to get up and take another step forward after repeatedly being knocked down.

• • •

The sun had just come up in Newcastle, a small town on the outskirts of Oklahoma City. It was November 7, 2014, and Donna Baldwin, forty-six, entered her nine-year-old son's bedroom. Riley was asleep on the bottom bunk. The top bunk was full of stuffed animals. Posters of Marvel superheroes hung from the walls. There was a giant beanbag chair in the corner next to stacks of Lego containers and a miniature table with video games on it. Donna took it all in. She tried not to think about the number ninety-two. But it was impossible not to.

"C'mon, Ri-Man, time to wake up."

Riley rubbed his eyes.

She sat on the edge of his bed and reminded him—no breakfast and no liquids. It was surgery day.

Riley knew the drill. He had been operated on ninety-one times. In a few hours he'd undergo throat surgery number ninety-two. He rolled out of bed and tried to look at the bright side. At least he didn't have to go to school.

He'd inherited his optimism from his mother. When confronted with adversity, Donna tended to see the glass half full. But in Riley's case, it was getting harder and harder to be positive. The hospital had become his home away from home.

> When confronted with adversity, Donna tended to see the glass half full.

It all started in June 2007, when Riley was two and a half. He was learning to speak. He knew his words, but something was wrong with his voice. He sounded like the Star Wars character Darth Vader. Only it wasn't an act. It was constant. Breathing was becoming a problem too.

Donna and her husband, Mark, a military veteran who worked in commercial construction, didn't know what to do. Riley had four older brothers—Dale, Dean, Lance, and Cooper. None of them had experienced anything similar. Riley's condition put them in unfamiliar territory. Worried, they took him to see a throat specialist.

Tests and X-rays revealed that Riley had recurrent respiratory papillomatosis. Donna had never heard of it. Sitting in a medical office, she squeezed Riley's hand as the doctor explained that it was a rare disease also known as laryngeal papillomatosis, or RRP, for short. It entailed the growth of tumors in the respiratory tract, primarily in the larynx and around the vocal chords. There are roughly twenty thousand cases in the U.S. There is no cure for RRP. The treatment is to surgically remove the tumors.

Donna had many questions, starting with "What happens after surgery?"

The doctor explained that the tumors would resurface, hence the term *recurrent*. Riley would need subsequent surgeries to remove them.

How long would this go on?

The doctor said he hoped the tumors would stop growing once Riley's immune system developed, perhaps by the time he was five or six, but it was hard to say one way or the other.

Donna held Riley on her lap and rocked him. There was so much to absorb, but there was no time for contemplation. Riley's tumors were so large, the doctor explained, that they were obstructing his airway. The opening wasn't much bigger than the tip of a ballpoint pen. He required immediate surgery to help him breathe.

They scheduled his surgery at Children's Hospital in Oklahoma City the next week. Donna held back the tears as Riley was put under general anesthesia and operated on for the first time. It took just under an hour to scrape away and remove the tumors. When he woke up in the recovery room, he had a low-grade fever and his throat was sore. But the first thing he asked for was a Nutter Butter cookie.

His voice was noticeably better. That lasted for about two weeks. Then the Darth Vader voice returned. On July 20, 2007, he had his second surgery. A month after that he had another.

Riley was too young to understand what was happening. His older brothers didn't get it either, but they wanted to do something to help. Donna convinced them that the best thing they could do was pray and have faith that the disease wouldn't spread beyond Riley's larynx.

> "We went to church every Sunday. I read the Bible, prayed, and asked for guidance. Faith, to me, is huge."

"I was brought up Methodist," Donna explained. "We went to church every Sunday. I read the Bible, prayed, and asked for guidance. Faith, to me, is huge. That's what I teach my boys."

• • •

Riley had undergone more than forty throat surgeries by the time he turned five. His family had gotten used to his alternating voices—soft one week, raspy the next. But when it came time for Riley to start kindergarten, Donna and Mark were worried that his classmates would ridicule him. Donna went with him on the first day of school. Before the start of class, she stood and addressed the children. "Hello, class," she began. "I'm Riley's mom."

She went on to explain that everybody in the class was unique. There were various hair colors and different heights and weights amongst the students. "God makes us different," she continued. "Differences make us special. Riley has a special voice."

Then she described it. The kids nodded.

"So, if sometimes you think it's hard to hear him," she said, "just ask him to speak up. He does the best he can."

Riley was easy to like, and the children embraced him. They'd wished him luck every six weeks when he had to miss school to undergo another surgery. The trips to the hospital had become so common that Donna and Riley referred to them as "Surgery Day." On those days Riley got to skip school because it was his special day. He got to be the boss and do fun things with Mom at the hospital. To lighten the mood and take Riley's mind off the procedures, Donna would refer to hospital gowns as costumes.

One time as Riley was slipping into his costume, he said to his mother, "Now you have to put on your costume, Mom." She laughed and put on a gown and a funny hat. Then she accompanied Riley into the operating room. She'd been there so many times the hospital staff treated her like part of the team.

As Riley lay down on the surgery table, the nurse asked: "What flavor today, Riley?"

"Watermelon."

Then, while softly singing his favorite song, "Dancing Bears," Donna gently placed the anesthesia mask over Riley's mouth and nose. She sang until his eyes widened, indicating that the watermelon-scented anesthesia was penetrating his tiny body. When he began to struggle, she steadied the mask until his eyes closed and he lost consciousness.

The nurses thanked her, and she retreated to the waiting room. Mark was there to greet her. "How'd it go?" he said.

She hesitated. Most days she kept her emotions in check, but when she watched Riley drift off under anesthesia that day, she couldn't help wondering if something would go wrong this time.

Forty-five minutes later, she went to the recovery room and waited by Riley's side. When he woke up, she gave him liquids through a straw to soothe his swollen throat. Five hours later they drove home. Surgery Day was over.

• • •

Riley completed kindergarten in the spring of 2011. His grandmother visited as soon as the school year ended. She was in the living room with Donna when the television weatherman began talking about a severe tornado headed toward Newcastle. All residents were urged to seek shelter underground. It was Tuesday, May 24. Mark came home from work early and told everyone to gather their personal belongings and get to the shelter.

He hurried the family underground just in time. The tornado was upon them just as he locked the cellar door.

It sounded like a freight train rumbling overhead. The extreme air pressure caused everyone's ears to fill and then pop. Objects slammed against the cellar door.

"Mom, can we pray?" Riley whispered.

"Of course," she said.

The family huddled together on a bench seat. Riley offered the prayer. "Please help us to all be okay," he said.

As soon as he said amen, another gust rumbled overhead, followed by an eerie silence. Mark pushed open the door. The first thing he noticed was that the door to the detached garage was gone. But the sight of another approaching twister instantly drew his attention. He slammed the door and climbed back down. Scared, everyone huddled and winced as a horrific sound came from above. They froze until the silence returned.

Mark pushed the door open again. "Well," he said, "the detached garage is gone."

Donna climbed the cellar stairs to see for herself. The missing garage was just the beginning. Both cars had been flipped around and flattened. The dog kennel was missing, and so were the dogs. A pile of rubble—mainly lumber and metal—stood where the kennel had been.

Mark called for the dogs. Nothing.

Crying, Donna yelled over her shoulder to her mother. "Keep the kids in the cellar."

Mark started digging through the rubble. Suddenly their black lab, Boomer, emerged. Then Donna heard a faint whimper. The other two dogs were trapped but alive. Neighbors helped rescue the dogs.

> "I believe God only gives us what we can handle," she explained. "I don't just crumble in the face of adversity. I push on. I will find a way no matter what."

Then Mark and Donna approached their brick house. It was still standing, but the roof had been blown off and the windows looked like they had been hit by machine-gun fire. Every one of them was shattered. Mark and Donna went inside, stepping over broken glass and busted wood and sheetrock. Donna looked around, speechless. The upstairs bedroom doors were in a heap on the first floor. The walls were demolished. A few personal items were salvageable. The house wasn't.

"Where will we live, Mom?" one of the boys said, having come out of the shelter.

Donna had no idea. But she told her boys not to worry. Everyone was alive. No one was hurt. They could deal with the rest.

"I believe God only gives us what we can handle," she

explained. "I don't just crumble in the face of adversity. I push on. I will find a way no matter what."

Mark and Donna took the family to a hotel. The rebuilding process began after the insurance company accessed the damages. Six months later, the house was rebuilt. The family moved back in just before Thanksgiving. They were in the midst of furnishing the place when Riley went in for another surgery.

At the same time, Donna encouraged her husband to have a mole on his arm checked. A dermatologist took a biopsy and sent it to the lab. The results came back on January 28, 2012. Mark had melanoma, stage three. He had just turned fifty. Based on what she could find online, Donna determined that Mark's chances of survival were less than 50 percent.

Donna tried to hold herself together but wondered why all this was happening to them. She couldn't help second-guessing her long-held belief that God didn't test people beyond their capacity to withstand. With all of Riley's surgeries and with the loss of their home, would she now lose her husband? Would she have to raise her boys on her own?

Afraid she'd sink into despair if she dwelled on the

> Afraid she'd sink into despair if she dwelled on the situation, she prayed for the strength and courage to stay positive.

situation, she prayed for the strength and courage to stay positive.

• • •

Within a two-week time frame in February, both Riley and Mark underwent surgery. Riley's went well. Mark's didn't. A few lymph nodes were removed from under his arm, but a week later doctors realized that the lymph nodes were cancerous, which required a second surgery in March. Mark nearly died during the second procedure. He ended up with a hole the size of a softball in his upper arm. Skin was taken from his leg to cover it. The residual pain from the graft was so intense that Mark sometimes collapsed in agony.

Donna spent weeks changing his dressings and helping him to the bathroom. He couldn't even dress himself. A month later, the chemotherapy started. Nurses warned that his hair would fall out and he'd lose weight. Trying to remain upbeat, Donna joked that he was already balding and could stand to lose a few pounds.

But the chemo killed Mark's appetite altogether. He dropped so much weight that none of his clothes fit him. Three months after the surgeries, he was still so weak he couldn't return to his job in construction work. He barely left the house anymore.

Mark's boss was sympathetic and continued to pay him his full wage. Eventually Mark reached a point where he could make it to the job site, but physical labor was too taxing. He had to take multiple naps while at work just to make it through each day. It was becoming increasingly clear that Mark had to find another job, one that wasn't so physically demanding.

At the same time, Donna was dragging. In addition to working full time as a legal assistant at a law office, she had to care for a sick husband and a child in need of constant trips to the hospital. Plus, she had other children at home. If Mark's condition didn't improve soon, she didn't see how they could make ends meet. There was still a lot of work to be done on the outside of their rebuilt home. It was all stuff Mark could do, like erecting a fence around the swimming pool, but another round of chemotherapy landed him back in bed. The fencing material remained on pallets in the back yard.

On May 10, 2012, Donna logged onto her Facebook page and started writing.

> I wonder sometimes how strong God thinks I am to continue to face trials. In the last 12 months I have had an emergency visit to have my appendix out; then, 2 weeks later a tornado destroys our house; we build it back in 4 months and then two months after that we find out my husband is diagnosed with Melanoma Skin Cancer stage 3. . . . During that time my son just had his 69th surgery

to keep his airways open. . . . I know He is in control and this is his plan for me, but I'm just curious how strong He thinks I am.

The boys couldn't help worrying about all the pressure on Donna. She kept telling them that life was like a game of cards—you had to play the cards you were dealt. But privately she had reached a breaking point. More than anything she needed the reassurance that God hadn't forgotten her, something to indicate that her prayers had been heard.

> "I know He is in control and this is his plan for me, but I'm just curious how strong He thinks I am."

Then, one Saturday, all the fathers from Riley's Little League team showed up at the Baldwin home. Tools in hand, the ten men started working on the fence. With tears in her eyes, Donna helped Mark to the patio and situated him in a chair that faced the volunteers. A few hours later the fence was up.

The mothers from the Little League team organized meals for the Baldwins. Each night a different family showed up at the doorstep with hot food. It was a clear indication to Donna that she was not alone.

Then Mark received a job offer to work for a private contractor. It wasn't as physically demanding, but there was still no way he could accept the position in his current condition. Desperate, Mark and Donna prayed. Afterward they concluded that Mark had to stop chemotherapy, otherwise he'd never have the strength to work again. Mark met with his oncologist, who warned them against the potential risks of discontinuing chemotherapy. But after having undergone seven months of chemo, Mark's ability to provide for his family was minimal at best, and so the decision was made.

Two weeks after stopping chemo, Mark started to regain his strength. He took the new job, and Donna turned her full attention back to Riley.

• • •

About the time Mark returned to work full time, Donna was tucking Riley into bed one night. He was now eight years old and had undergone approximately eighty surgeries.

Donna was running her hand through his hair when he looked at her and asked, "Mom, why did God give me this voice?"

She hesitated, thinking, *I have to be strong for my son.*

"You know, Riley, maybe one day you will have this cool job where you can do voice-overs with your cool, special voice. Who knows?"

Seeming satisfied with her answer, he closed his eyes and nodded off.

As she turned out the light and stared at him, she started to question why God had given him that voice. *Why?*

Then she thought about the many other children she'd seen at the hospital who were worse off than Riley. She immediately counted her blessings.

Donna tried to count her blessings when the doctor spoke with her following Riley's ninety-second surgery on November 14, 2014. There had been a setback, he told her. The papillomas had spread to Riley's esophagus.

Donna knew one other boy who had tumors in his esophagus. The tumors had spread to the boy's lungs, and he'd had to undergo chemotherapy. After what Mark had gone through, there was no way she wanted Riley to experience chemo.

> "God has blessed us," said Donna. "And I know He expects us to fight."

There was one other option, the doctor said. Shortening the time in between surgeries would prevent the tumors from reaching his esophagus. Instead of every six weeks, Riley would undergo surgery every five weeks.

Donna talked it over with Mark, then they did what they always do. They prayed. And they pushed forward.

"When this disease started to attack his body in 2007, we never thought the number of surgeries would get to one hundred," she said. On November 17, 2015, Riley Baldwin had his one hundredth surgery, then he went home and played his new Disney Infinity video game.

"God has blessed us," said Donna. "And I know He

expects us to fight." She laughed and added, "The Baldwins aren't going down without fight. For sure, we will be strong and press forward until Riley's immune system can fight off the papillomas more easily. We will be strong no matter what adversity comes our way."

Donna Baldwin had read Dr. Seuss stories to Riley from the time he was very young. These words of wisdom from Dr. Seuss are particularly applicable when it comes to Donna and her "can do" attitude: "I learned there are troubles of more than one kind. Some come from the head, others come from behind. But I've brought a big bat. I'm all ready, you see. Now my troubles are going to have trouble with me."

Donna Baldwin certainly has run into troubles of more than one kind, some of which have knocked her down a time or two. But she's chosen to get back up, step up to the plate, and swing the bat. Her grit is a powerful call to those who feel beaten down: "Get up and choose to be strong!"

"We grow morally as a consequence of learning how to be with others, how to behave in this world, a learning prompted by taking to heart what we have seen and heard."

—ROBERT COLES

CHAPTER SEVEN

Choose to Be a *Mighty Good Parent*

Robert Coles is a Pulitzer Prize–winning author and an emeritus professor of psychiatry and medical humanities at the Harvard Medical School. He's published more than eighty books, most of which explore moral, social, and spiritual reasoning in children. His groundbreaking book, *The Moral Intelligence of Children*, was prompted by research he'd done on the disparity between character and intellect. He concluded that "moral intelligence" isn't acquired only by memorization of rules and regulations or by dint of classroom discussion or kitchen compliance. "We grow morally as a consequence of learning how to be with others, how to behave in this world, a learning prompted by taking to heart what we have seen and heard."

It's not surprising that parents are the primary influence in a child's development of moral intelligence. Coles wrote: "The child is witness; the child is an ever-attentive witness of grown-up morality—or lack thereof; the child looks and looks for cues as to how one ought to behave, and finds them galore as we parents and teachers go about our lives, making choices, addressing people, showing in action our rock-bottom assumptions, desires, and values, and thereby telling those young observers more than we may realize."

This is a story about two parents who dedicated their lives to instilling moral intelligence in their children. They are not simply good parents. They are mighty good parents.

• • •

On a Friday afternoon in September 2011, a bus arrived at Compton High School in Southern California with rival Dominguez High's football team aboard. I was there to cover the game for a *Sports Illustrated* story I was writing on high school football and street gangs. During warm-ups I approached the best player on the Compton team, eighteen-year-old Kitam Hamm Jr., and asked him what he wanted to be when he grew up. I expected him to say a professional football player. He said a lawyer. Curious, I asked about his grades. His GPA was a 3.8, he told me, and he had offers to play football at Harvard, Stanford, Princeton, and Columbia.

Compton is home to thirty-four active street gangs.

Most high school-age boys there have had some association with a gang or a run-in with gang members. One of the football coaches told me that there was a lot of pressure on his players to join gangs.

"Have you ever been tempted to join a gang?" I asked Kitam.

"No," he said. "My father would kill me."

"Will your father be at the game tonight?"

"My father is at all of my games."

"Where can I find him?"

"He'll be sitting with my mom."

That evening I found Kitam Hamm Sr. and his wife, Donyetta, in the bleachers. I introduced myself and told them how impressed I was with their son. When they shared their story with me, I was so taken with what I was hearing that I decided to write an entirely different story. I asked their permission to profile them and their son in *Sports Illustrated*. They agreed. A few weeks later I flew back to Compton and essentially moved into their apartment. They set up a cot for me in Kitam Jr.'s bedroom, and I went everywhere with him. I attended all of

> Their family was a testament of their commitment to one another and of their determination to endure and overcome obstacles that were well beyond my life's experience.

his classes, including a voluntary Bible study class that met during the lunch hour.

In December 2011, *Sports Illustrated* published "Straight Outta Compton," Kitam Jr.'s story. By then I had developed tremendous admiration for Kitam Sr. and Donyetta. In a difficult environment foreign to most Americans, the Hamms had developed a model marriage and raised four children, three of whom had gone on to college. Their family was a testament of their commitment to one another and of their determination to endure and overcome obstacles that were well beyond my life's experience. Donyetta thanked me for writing about her son, but I thanked her for letting me into their lives. I'm a better person as a result.

• • •

The iPhone beside Kitam Hamm's bed vibrated at 6:15 one morning in late October 2011. A car alarm pulsed in the alley below, and police sirens screamed past. Squinting, the eighteen-year-old high school senior sat up and flipped on the light. It was just before dawn in Compton.

Kitam started his day by confronting things most teenage boys don't even have to think about when getting ready for school: *What should I wear?* For Kitam, the answer is complicated by the fact that his street represents a border between rival neighborhood street gangs. Colors, particularly of shirts and baseball caps, can signify affiliation and invite peril. He flipped through his closet until settling on a plaid shirt and dark pair of jeans. Then he went to the kitchen, plugged in the iron, and pressed his clothes. Ironing was part of his morning routine, a habit he learned from his mother. Appearance, she taught him, mattered.

Kitam had just finished when his parents, Kitam Sr. and Donyetta, both thirty-nine, entered the kitchen. His father prepared breakfast. His mother made sure Kitam was ready for school. A video monitor on the kitchen counter carried a live feed from a security camera positioned at the entrance gate outside their twelve-unit apartment complex.

It was almost seven thirty when Kitam Jr. slung his book bag over his shoulder, said good-bye to his mother, and followed his dad to the car.

Kitam Sr. drove his son to school every day. No exceptions. When Kitam Jr. had started high school, he had relied on public transportation to get to and from school. But one afternoon he stepped off a city bus across the street from his home, and two young men approached him. One had a gun.

"Where you from, Blood?" the one with the gun said, gang speak for "What gang are you in?"

Kitam froze and quickly remembered the lessons his father had drilled into him: *Don't act hard. Remain calm. Give the right answer.*

"Nowhere," Kitam told the armed man. "I ain't from nowhere," code for "I'm not in a gang."

That answer saved his life. The gangster stared him

down, then tucked his gun into his waistband, and moved on. Kitam collapsed on the bus-stop bench, knowing he had just dodged a bullet—literally.

After that, Kitam gladly accepted daily rides from his father. Their route was a familiar one, down streets lined with billboards and small businesses with barred windows. A nail salon. A package store. An automotive repair shop. Kitam Sr. often used the ten-minute commute to give his son a pep talk or share some advice.

On this particular morning, the topic was football. Kitam—a five foot nine inch, 170-pound running back and defensive back—was the best player on his high school team. With Leo Sayer's "Oh Girl" playing on the radio in the background, Kitam Sr. explained the importance of using leverage to compensate for his lack of size when tackling opposing players. Kitam Jr. said he'd be able to hit even harder if he were heavier.

> "Size matters," his father told him. "Don't get me wrong. But if you're small and you're strong, you can still rock a person."

"Size matters," his father told him. "Don't get me wrong. But if you're small and you're strong, you can still rock a person."

These morning talks were part of a special father-son bond that grew out of Kitam Sr.'s goal to teach his son right from wrong, as well as how to survive on the streets. He'd been protecting and teaching his son for years. When Kitam

Jr. was twelve, his father started taking him to a neighbor-hood basketball court to play with older kids, forcing him to find ways to get his shot off against the taller, stronger players. One day a man in a hooded sweatshirt showed up. Kitam Sr. sensed he was armed. Moments later the man was pointing that gun at one of the players. "Stay behind me," Kitam Sr. told his son. Then he raised his hands and stepped toward the armed man. "Please don't kill this guy in front of my son," he pleaded. "My son don't need to see this." After a tense pause, the gunman left, and Kitam Sr. took his son home.

"If you want to know how bad and dirty it is, all you have to do is pay attention to where we live and how many guys are ending up dead," Kitam Sr. explained. "The gangs don't care about kids or how old or young you are. You have to stay away and not get caught up by being in the wrong place at the wrong time."

The message got through to Kitam Jr. When his father dropped him off at the gates outside Compton High, he hustled to his first class. School didn't start for another thirty minutes. He used the time to take down all thirty-five chairs the janitor had left on the desks. Then he looked over his homework. He could hear his mother's words—*Don't waste time. Keep busy.* Those instructions helped him establish a 3.8 GPA. They also kept him out of trouble, especially during lunch hour.

Compton High has about 2,400 students. At lunch,

hundreds of them avoid the cafeteria, choosing instead to hang out in the school's sunny courtyard. The atmosphere resembles an outdoor block party. Kitam wasn't interested in hanging out. Instead, he'd recruit friends to accompany him to a classroom adjacent to the courtyard. Inside, a representative from the Fellowship of Christian Athletes read from the Bible while about forty students listened in. "Being tempted is not a sin," the representative told them. "It's how you respond to temptation that matters."

> Kitam would recruit friends to accompany him to a classroom adjacent to the courtyard. Inside, a representative from the Fellowship of Christian Athletes read from the Bible.

Kitam never missed the Bible study sessions. He was the student-leader of the Bible group. Many of the kids he recruited to the class were his football teammates and some of the cheerleaders. They went because Kitam went. Kitam went because his mother had taught him the importance of having the Lord in his life.

"Faith has gotten us through a lot of hard things," Donyetta explained. "It's not easy living where we live. We've worked very hard to raise our family a certain way. At the same time, I want my son to acknowledge the hand of God in his life."

Donyetta was raised Baptist. As a little girl she attended church every Sunday with her grandmother. One of her best memories was listening to her grandmother sing gospel hymns while preparing meals in the kitchen. Her grandmother also taught her the importance of prayer. "Early on I learned that praying made me feel better," she said. "So I taught my kids to pray."

So much of the Hamms' approach to parenting stemmed from their upbringing. Donyetta and Kitam Sr. met in 1987 when they were both fifteen. He was affiliated with a gang and selling drugs. Donyetta soon got pregnant. By sixteen they had a child and were on welfare. Then Kitam Sr. ended up in a juvenile detention center. While he was incarcerated, Donyetta found out she was pregnant with their second child. When Kitam got released, she put her foot down—no more gangs, no more crime, get a real job.

> "Early on I learned that praying made me feel better," she said. "So I taught my kids to pray."

"Donyetta changed my thinking," Kitam Sr. explained. "All my friends were going to jail, so it wasn't hard for me to walk away. But my dad used drugs, and I didn't have the proper structure to teach me how to provide for my children. I just decided I wanted my kids to grow up and be part of a solution and not part of a problem."

Kitam Sr. got a job unloading trucks at a warehouse. He and Donyetta were twenty-one when Kitam Jr. came along. By that time the Hamms also had three daughters. Financially, the situation was bleak. But Kitam Sr. resisted the pressure to return to the gang. Instead, he worked tirelessly at the warehouse. "That's how he provided for his family for years," Donyetta said. "He had to butt heads with a lot of gang members. He had numerous fights. But he was determined to be with me and our children. It's amazing we made it. We fought to be where we are today."

> "I've had many bad and horrible instances in my life. But the good experiences have been so powerful that they overshadow the bad ones. And they remind me that God doesn't give me challenges beyond my ability to overcome."

Donyetta regularly wore a small cross on her necklace to remind her of Jesus. She'd kiss it when she felt overwhelmed or scared. There were plenty of days when she wondered if she'd make it. She even questioned whether God had overestimated her strength. "I'd often say, 'God, how strong do you think I am?' I've had many bad and horrible instances in my life. But the good experiences have been so powerful that they overshadow the bad ones. And they remind me that God doesn't give me challenges beyond my ability to overcome."

· · ·

The Hamms were a model family. Their three daughters were solid students at Compton High; two continued on to college. Kitam Jr. was a model student, a star athlete, and a humble leader among his peers. He'd also managed not to get hurt or be influenced by the presence of street gangs.

"Having a father in the home makes a big difference," Kitam Sr. said. "A lot of kids here don't have dads, and a gang becomes their only family. I told Kitam early on that before I allow a gang to take you out, I'll take you out first. The only gang Kitam belongs in is the Hamm family."

Galvanized by their own childhood experiences, Donyetta and Kitam Sr. did everything possible to protect Kitam Jr. from the influences of the street. "We live in Blood territory, and there have been a lot of murders here," Donyetta said. "We don't let Kitam go anywhere without permission. He comes home from football practice, and we eat together as a family every night. Then he does his homework. He's not allowed out after dark. He has a very structured life."

> "We go through life believing there is a higher power, something greater than us. It's believing in something we can't see. That's what faith is."

Faith is a major component of that structure. "I am not a perfect parent," Donyetta said. "My husband and I do our best. We go through life believing there is a higher power, something greater than us. It's believing in something we can't see. That's what faith is. And we've tried to instill that in Kitam and our daughters."

. . .

It was dark by the time football practice ended. A tired Kitam Jr. emerged from the locker room and went straight to the car. His father was parked in the same spot where he always waited. When they got home, Donyetta had dinner waiting—oven-baked enchiladas. It was after nine by the time Kitam headed to his room. He had to write an essay to go along with one of his college applications. Notepad in hand, he sat on his bed, put his earbuds in, and scrolled through his iTunes library to his favorite song, "Bless the Broken Road," by Rascal Flatts. He raised the volume and mouthed the words: "*I set out on a narrow way many years ago, hoping I would find true love along the broken road. . . . This much I know is true, that God blessed the broken road.*"

The lyrics fit how he felt toward his parents—they had overcome a lot, and he had been blessed by God to be their son.

With his parents in the next room, he began writing the essay. He began with what it felt like when he'd first learned a decade earlier that his mother had Hodgkin's lymphoma. The words came easily.

> When I was 7 years old I found out what cancer was. Being so young I really didn't know how to handle the situation. Only thing I can remember is every time the subject came up, people got quiet and tears started to fall.

He kept writing until his bedroom door opened and Donyetta poked her head in. She wanted to know how he was progressing on his college application. He said he was almost done with his essay. She wanted to see it. Reluctant, he handed her his pad, afraid she might not like it.

Donyetta didn't like to talk about her cancer. It had been in remission for years. But it had recently returned, and she was undergoing chemotherapy. She avoided the topic on account that she didn't want people to think she was weak. She wasn't looking for pity.

Silently she read the essay and handed it back. "I love you," she told him. "Good night."

"Good night, Mom."

He hadn't said "I love you," but she knew. On his eighteenth birthday, Kitam had come home and told her he had gotten a tattoo on his chest. Donyetta had strictly forbidden tattoos. But when he lifted his shirt, she couldn't scold him. The tattoo read "Donyetta."

She closed his bedroom door. It was a few minutes past

> "You can't always choose your circumstances or what happens to you in life," Donyetta always said. "But you can choose to live your life the way Jesus did."

midnight. Exhausted, Kitam set the alarm on his iPhone for 6:15. Then he turned out the light, clasped his hands, looked up, and prayed before going to sleep: "God, please keep me safe."

In the next room, Donyetta slid into bed, satisfied. Her son was one day closer to graduating. Her son was safe. Her son had faith. He trusted them.

"You can't always choose your circumstances or what happens to you in life," Donyetta always said. "But you can choose to live your life the way Jesus did."

• • •

After graduating from Compton High in 2012, Kitam Jr. enrolled in college. On January 1, 2015, he posted this on his Facebook page:

> This last year I can really say the devil tried to break me. I went through a lot of trials and tribulations and I'm still standing. This past year I dealt with a lot of depression and cloudy days. At times I felt like giving up and I didn't want to be here anymore. But the God I worship and praise wouldn't

let me. He showed me where there's a will there's a way.

God didn't promise days without pain, laughter without sorrow, or sun without rain. But He did promise strength for the day, comfort for the tears, and light for the way. If God brings you to it, He will bring you through it.

He is expected to graduate in 2016.

Donyetta and Kitam Sr. celebrated their twentieth wedding anniversary in 2015. They attend worship services every Sunday at a church near their home. They are now forty-three. "At this point in my life," Donyetta said, "I don't question God anymore. My faith is strong. And when things go bad I pray until something good happens."

When I think of the Hamm family, I can't help but see the results of the hard work of mighty good parents. Raising a family today is tough. Raising kids who are, as Dr. Robert Coles pointed out, "courteous, compassionate, caring, warm-hearted, and unpretentious" is even tougher. It's no coincidence that Kitam Jr. made it through his teen years and graduated unscathed by gangs, drugs, or peer pressure. I'm an eyewitness of the things his parents did day in and day out to ensure that Kitam was grounded in family and faith. They did things

> "When things go bad I pray until something good happens."

like eat together and practice the lifestyle Jesus teaches in the Bible. Most important, Kitam knew he was loved. That was evident in the simple things, such as the daily car rides to and from school when his father would talk to him about everything from football to fatherhood. And Donyetta set firm family rules and expressed her faith to Kitam regularly, and her husband backed her up. It's easy to see the "mighty good" parenting they did. It was a choice.

I think of myself as a good parent, but the examples of Kitam Sr. and Donyetta inspire me to want to be a mighty good parent.

AFTERWORD

Actor Michael J. Fox once said, "I have no choice about whether or not I have Parkinson's. I have nothing but choices about how I react to it. In those choices, there's freedom to do a lot of things in areas that I wouldn't have otherwise found myself in."

For most of us, choice is a constant. In this book I've shared seven stories of people who've purposely chosen to live happier, more abundant lives.

The choice to forgive can free us from our personal prisons. Just ask Hugh.

The choice to give someone a second chance is more than just forgiving them—it's going above and beyond to help that person, even when they have hurt you. Bruce did that.

The choice to serve others is a powerful step away from crushing sadness toward true joy. Just ask Scott and Icy.

The choice to believe allows us to have a life-changing relationship with God. Lindsay chose to believe.

Choosing to exercise prayer allows God to perform miracles in our lives. Kev and Judith demonstrate that.

The choice to be strong gives you the willpower to get up and keep going, no matter what. It's in Donna's DNA.

The choice to be a mighty good parent doesn't mean you have to be perfect. And it doesn't mean your child will necessarily turn out the way you've dreamed or supposed. However, a mighty good parent who chooses to teach moral intelligence to a child gives them a gift far more valuable than intellect or wealth. Just ask Kitam Sr. and Donyetta.

The people in this book and their stories and examples have had a profound influence on me. I'm a better person because of my association with them. Their choices have inspired me to choose a happier, more abundant life and to realize that in spite of—and maybe even because of—trials and challenges, life can be mighty good.